To the
Pleasant
Middle
Librarian

A Handful of Flowers

❧

Barry Holcomb

Barry Holcomb

Keep on reading!

ISBN: 1499251394
ISBN-13: 9781499251395

Foreword

Welcome, readers, one and all. I present before you a smorgasbord; there should be something here to suit your taste, no matter your age, gender, or persuasion. We have bits and pieces of history, stories of success and glory, and stories of terrific blunder. Some pieces are purely tongue-in-cheek, and you will read of pranks pulled and yarns told.

The book's title comes from a true story you will find hidden deep within these pages. Each little tale stands as a single flower, a story in and of itself. Individually the stories are short and small; combined, they make a grand bouquet and tell a greater story.

You will meet a variety of people between the pages, hopefully see the handiwork of the Almighty. As I finalized this book I struggled to achieve the correct balance between strict reporting of verifiable facts and the telling of events as I remembered and understood them. You will hear mentions of faith and of prayer; to tell the stories honestly, faith must be included.

To fully experience these stories you will take a trip in my time machine. Events are not necessarily in chronological order; buckle on your seatbelt for a bumpy ride. One peculiar feature of this book is that each chapter is a story in and of itself; some stories intersect and overlap. An event described in great detail in one chapter may be mentioned briefly in another, from a completely different perspective. There is no attempt to tell you how to live your life. I speak from my heart and my experience; and I am FAR from perfect.

The stories come from several sources. My writing began almost 40 years ago when I was just 17. Some of the shortest pieces appeared in *The Clinton Chronicle*. Others written for *The Beacon* of Selma, Alabama. Others were printed in *The Westmoreland News* of Virginia. One appeared in a publication by the Broadman Press, and a fair number appeared in a weekly column for an artists' community website. A few are making their debut.

My deepest thanks go to two relatives, both of whom are editors, and one I have never even met. Lynn Norris of Kinsale, Virginia, encouraged me for many months and assisted me in more ways than I can describe. You will get a wonderful view of her in "My Snowglobe on the Shelf." Karen Glenn, a cousin and beloved story-teller to my wife as a child, helped give structure and sharpen the view. She is mentioned briefly in "The Camel's Final Journey." To both ladies I extend my deepest thanks.

As a teenager I discovered and fell in love with the writings of Erma Bombeck. She possessed equal abilities to make me bust a gut laughing or to suddenly pause and shed a tear. Her talents did not appear until she was an adult and mother of teenagers; this yielded much encouragement to me. The sarcasm and dry wit of Andy Rooney also added a pinch of flavor to my style which brewed for years slowly on a back burner. Some years ago I was enthralled by the movie *I Remember Mama*. You may notice some similarities in this volume to that film. Even today I take great pleasure in viewing this wonderfully composed reverie.

But there is yet another woman whose talents helped bring this book into existence. Without her guidance, none of it would ever have been written. You will meet her between the pages; without a doubt you will recognize her story.

So sit back and enjoy this little experiment in literature. You may consume a large slice as you sit back and enjoy it with a cup of hot tea, or you may relish it like a box of special chocolates, consuming only a story at a time. If I can make you smile, bring a tear to your eye, maybe make you laugh out loud a time or two, if I can make you think of the hereafter, then I have accomplished my mission.

Thank you, for the opportunity to weave a tale for you. I truly hope you find enjoyment in the contents.

CONTENTS

CHAPTER 1

Carol

I Guess You'll Have to Import Me One

Tom and Joyce Campbell and I were talking after Share Group, a home Bible study which was still going strong after more than five years. My sophomore year of college was almost complete. Most of my friends were talking about plans for the summer.

Everyone had someone special, a boyfriend or girlfriend, everyone but me. I had dated some during high school; I had even gone out with some of the girls at Share Group. But we always ended up only being good friends; the romantic spark just wasn't there.

When I described my loneliness Joyce had an answer. "Ask God to IMPORT someone for you. That's what I did!" She described how she had felt the same way in her hometown of Miami. She could not find the right person and prayed God would IMPORT him for her. Tom was serving in the Air Force and was soon reassigned to Miami; they met at church and had a head-over-heels romance. They were very happily married and had a beautiful daughter. The formula had worked for her; it couldn't hurt to try.

Throughout the hot dry summer I made frequent requests that God would import the right girl for me. When the fall term started at Presbyterian College, there were plenty of new students. At lunch one day I met Carol, a freshman from Atlanta; she was talking with a member of the campus Bible study. We did not hit it off well. She thought I was a country hick, and I considered her a city snob.

We passed on campus, nodding but keeping our distance. However, when we attended a retreat, we ended up sitting beside each other. Enthralled with the speaker, we listened intently, flipping through our Bibles to follow his references. Side by side, we could not help but notice we had underlined the same verses time and again. After the lecture, we began to talk earnestly. Soon we were amazed at the similarities in our lives. We spent every spare minute of the weekend opening our hearts and sharing with each other.

We both sang in the college choir. The following Monday I hurried to arrive at practice before her, placing a single yellow rose on her seat. She picked it up affectionately, turning to find the sender. I looked at the ceiling and blushed. She, too, blushed and turned away.

I asked Carol to join me for a movie at the Broadway the following Friday. Meeting me at her dormitory door, she asked, "Where is your car?" She was surprised when I replied we could walk to the theatre. Coming from Atlanta, she was nervous about walking anywhere after dark. I explained that Clinton was a small town, and we would be perfectly safe.

We spent so much time together that I wonder now how we completed our course work. I taught her how to drive a stick-shift, and we forever laughed at her struggles to master the clutch and shifting gears.

She was my first love. I found myself falling head over heels for this beautiful young woman. Soon, we became concerned that we were drawing too close too fast. We agreed to try dating others to see how we both felt.

The following Friday we went on separate dates. She was going out with a friend of mine. I had asked Cheryl, another girl on Carol's hall, to accompany me to Greenville for a movie. As we sat enjoying a snack afterwards, I realized I was doing Cheryl a terrible injustice; the entire evening I had spoken non-stop about Carol. We drove back to the dorm, where I thanked Cheryl for the evening, and stopped at the desk. I asked the monitor to tell Carol to call me the instant she returned.

Within thirty minutes we met under one of the tall oak trees outside her dorm. I told her how my date had gone, and she had been absolutely miserable on her outing. We agreed we never wanted to date anyone else ever again.

It was too early for an engagement; I still had two years of college, and she was just a freshman. But my sense of responsibility drove me to do something out of the ordinary. I asked Carol for her parents' names and mailing address. I wrote them a letter, introducing myself and explaining that we were dating. I promised them my intentions were honorable.

Over the next two years I came to love her parents, as well; occasionally we would drive to Atlanta to visit for the weekend. We shared picnics, homemade ice cream, cookouts and trips to Stone Mountain. Back at school, we continued to see each other constantly. One of our favorite diversions was to walk several blocks towards town to watch the trains pass. I signed her first valentine, "I love you train-loads." Trains and yellow roses became important throughout our life together.

When Carol and I first met, I had forgotten my prayers for God to import someone for me. Tom and Joyce came to know Carol and saw how attached we were becoming. It was over a year before we announced our engagement to the Share Group. Joyce pulled my sleeve and whispered into my ear, "I told you He would import someone for you."

Carol and the Roller Coaster

It was July of 1975. Carol was at home from college during the summer break. I was taking three classes at Erskine College to squeeze in needed credits to graduate from Presbyterian the following June. Carol was busily working as a keypunch operator at a national data credit center.

I had a couple of days break for the 4th of July and drove to Atlanta for a short visit. We were looking forward to a romp at Six Flags.

I had always enjoyed roller coasters and thrill rides; Carol was petrified of them. During the drive, she talked about some of the shows at Six Flags, but my goal was to ride The Great American Scream Machine, their largest coaster. Carol assured me I could not even drag her onto the ride, but she would wait while I enjoyed it. Somehow, my enthusiasm piqued her curiosity.

Once we entered the gate, Carol forgot about her plans to work our way slowly around the park. "Let's go look at it," she said with excitement as she pulled me towards the giant coaster.

As we stood surveying the 42-foot tall structure, I grew excited about the breathtaking ride to come. Dancing with excitement, she looked into my eyes. "Let's RIDE it!"

I grinned as I watched her during the wait. All through the zigzag queue, she alternated between anticipation and nervousness. Finally, we sat and the safety bar lowered and locked. Instantly the look of excitement faded from her face. The car started rolling, slowly creeping away from the platform. She was already screaming.

I tried to calm her, patting her on the knee. "Calm down, Honey. Nothing has happened YET." Her knuckles were white as she clasped the safety bar with all her might. Soon the steep climb began, drawing us near the crest of the first hill.

The car reached the top and paused just a moment. Then the plummet began. I watched the tracks speeding towards us as we fell towards the ground. I heard no screams, but when I turned and looked, Carol was frozen in terror, her mouth open much wider than I thought possible.

As we sped along the tracks at ground level, THEN the screams came. Short bursts of "OW!" "OH!" and "Help Me!" were repeated until we began the climb of the next hill. Then she let out a loud long wail, "Let me get OFF!" From the crest of the hill all the way down she made one long scream.

We had passed the two big hills. We still had several short hills and jerks, punctuated by quick "Ow's" and "Oh's" until we finally rolled back to the starting point.

The bar rose, and I helped my wobbly sweetheart stand. "Oh, oh, oh," she moaned as I helped her to a bench. Suddenly she punched me in the shoulder. "Why did you let me do that!" she asked. "I can't believe you let me ride that thing!"

After a cooling drink and a few minutes rest, she regained her composure; we returned to her original plan, watching several shows and enjoying other non-terrifying rides. Throughout the day she repeated her disbelief that she had ridden the Great Scream Machine.

Finally, the day was drawing towards an end. We had enjoyed musical shows, watched porpoises perform, and had ridden a train and a carousel. We were only a few yards from the exit when she suddenly turned and pulled my arm. She stood nose to nose with me wearing a huge grin. "Let's go ride it AGAIN!"

Sing for your Supper

The Madrigal Dinner was always the biggest event in Clinton every December. Presbyterian College produced a dinner concert of songs and entertainment recreating a 16th-century English Christmas, and year after year the tickets for all performances sold out rapidly.

The entire college choir would participate in the performance. In September auditions were held, and 14 singers would be chosen to be the lords and ladies of the madrigal dinner. Two students would be chosen to train as the jester and the court magician. Others were selected for minstrels and dancers. The less talented were assigned to decorate the banquet hall and serve the guests. My roommate, George, Carol and her roommate, Elizabeth were all selected to be madrigals. I had to hang greenery and serve tables.

The lords and ladies practiced for months, learning the eight-part harmony of Christmas songs from the past. The dancers and minstrels practiced, learning different steps and songs to entertain the crowds who would attend the reservation-only concerts.

After months of preparation, the performances were actually happening. People arrived well in advance, waiting outside in the frosty air until the trumpeter signaled the opening of the great hall. Dressed in their holiday best, the guests entered and mingled with the lords and ladies and the jester. After enjoying hot mulled cider, the guests sat down to savor the period meal and experience a delightful performance of song, dance, magic, and merriment. It was no surprise that many returned year after year.

Throughout the colorful performance I was able to sip and nibble just a bit, but I watched as my friends sang under the hot lights. As the crowd enjoyed their drinks, roast beef, Yorkshire pudding, and delicious vegetables, the lords and ladies sang, only getting a sip of water between carols. They kept up their spirits and sang beautifully, despite their hunger and the perspiration trickling down their hot stiff costumes. The madrigals descended from the stage, joining the crowd and lifting the audience into a crescendo of good spirit as they all joined and sang the final carol of "*We Wish you a Merry Christmas.*"

At long last, the weeks of practice and the hours of performing were complete. The last few guests were exiting the hall as my friends turned to me. "Barry, we're starving. Is there anything left to eat?" I raced through the kitchen, but the staff had already packed everything away.

I looked at my watch. "It's 11:15 now. There's only one place open; we can get a hotdog at the Dairy Twirl." The girls wanted to get out of their costumes, but I interjected, "We don't have time. They close in 45 minutes."

So, two ladies and one lord in costume and I in my tux climbed into my VW beetle to drive eight miles to the Dairy Twirl in nearby Laurens.

We pulled up on the gravel lot of the Dairy Twirl; there were several other customers leaning against their cars as they ate their hotdogs and French fries. The customers stared in amazement as this mysterious group dressed in finery climbed out of a VW bug. George and I held the doors for the ladies and bowed as they exited my fine coach.

I approached the tiny window of Dairy Twirl to place the order as my noble companions awaited their dinner. The three hefty ladies inside stared in amazement at our garb as I ordered hotdogs, fries, and milkshakes for all of us. Elizabeth cooled herself a bit with her fan, as Carol read her program and George strutted about puffing on a pipe. A few cars passing on the road slowed to a crawl. The passengers leaned out their windows, staring at the strange group in Elizabethan costumes at a hot dog stand on a frigid Saturday night in December.

As I collected our order, the waitress leaned forward and ventured, "Uh, were y'all at a costume party or something?" Her two co-workers huddled close behind, just as curious as she.

"Oh, no," I responded. "We wear these outfits whenever we feel like singing. Would you like to hear?" The heavy set waitress nodded her head. The trio of performers stood erect and sang with gusto as I directed them in one verse of The Boar's Head Carol.

When we finished, the three ladies applauded, as customers in the parking lot tooted their horns and raised their Budweiser bottles in salute. We bowed and curtsied, climbed back into the Beetle, and drove away.

Patt, the Negotiator

I graduated in 1976, but Carol had two more years of study remaining. I had rented a small apartment, working third shift and sleeping during the day. It was more difficult to see Carol now, but we usually had some time together on the weekend.

Occasionally Carol would visit me in the afternoon and watch television. I had always been a sci-fi fan, so I was caught off guard when I learned she had never heard of Star Trek. The original episodes aired every afternoon, and soon she was hooked. In the years to come she would amass a collection of hundreds of Star Trek novels.

The physical attraction between us was growing stronger. We both wanted to remain chaste until marriage, but doing so was becoming a real struggle.

It was November of 1976. Carol and I had been discussing how we both wanted to marry. With Carol sitting on my lap, I picked up the phone and dialed her parents' number. In just a moment, her father answered. I got straight to the point. "Patt, are you sitting down? Okay, I'll wait."

Carol looked at me, not knowing what was going through my head, not yet. Patt assured me he was sitting down and ready for the news. "Patt, I want to marry your daughter."

Carol was shocked and giddy with excitement, only hearing my half of the conversation. I explained that it was getting too difficult to wait for Carol to graduate and that I wanted to marry her much sooner.

"Are you thinking of marrying next summer?" he asked. I thought Patt sounded surprisingly calm. I was prepared for a certain amount of disapproval.

"No," I replied. "I want her to take a break from school at the end of the semester. We can marry soon after Christmas. I will pay for her last year and a half of school."

Patt remained calm. He explained that he and Lillian really wanted her to finish college; he was afraid that I wouldn't be able to support us and pay for college. I felt confident that somehow I would.

Patt sounded serious but reasonable. I was anxious over the plan I was suggesting, but his calm reaction encouraged me. Patt suggested that we resume the conversation a little later. He was going to discuss my idea with Lillian; he would call me back shortly.

Carol was absolutely beside herself. She was so excited about the prospect of getting married, but she was afraid that her daddy would say no. I had developed a deep respect for this man. Neither of us wanted to be out of his good graces.

In half an hour Patt called me back. He and Lillian had discussed my plan, but she too feared that stopping mid-year would be a mistake. They both understood the desire to marry sooner and did not want to interfere with young love.

"I want to suggest a different plan," Patt said calmly. "Let Carol finish this school year. You can get married next summer." Uh-oh. I could see major roadblocks ahead.

But I waited to hear all Patt had to say. "Lillian really wants Carol to have a nice church wedding." This sounded like more delays. I was ready to get married at the courthouse. "If you can do this for us, we'll pay for the last two years of college."

My jaw dropped. He had just removed a huge burden. And he didn't say "No." Just wait a few more months? And they would pay for college? This was almost unbelievable.

Carol had watched my expressions, trying to figure out what was happening. Her hopes had fallen at first, but now she was puzzled.

I thanked Patt, telling him this was a much better plan. "Now, I need to talk this over with Carol, but I am sure we will be talking again REAL soon." Carol was stumped by the smug grin on my face.

I explained the new plan to Carol, and her jaw dropped just like mine. Before she had time to ask any new questions, I asked mine. "Will you marry me?"

She squealed and yelled, "Yes! Yes! Yes!" We kissed, and laughed, and kissed some more. Carol couldn't wait to get back to the dorm and tell all her friends.

"I'll call you tomorrow when I get up, Sweetie," I said as she approached the door. She turned and her entire face was beaming. "I'll come over and we'll go pick out a ring." She ran back and we kissed again before she left, floating out on a cloud.

I am NOT Moody!

During most of the pregnancy Carol did really well. It was a challenge for her sometimes to walk the three blocks to work. Her main complaint was having to go up and down the stairs of the apartment to use the bathroom frequently. Looking back on it we used to say she was always hungry, always sleepy, and always going to the bathroom.

She experienced short spells of morning sickness, but the old remedy of keeping Saltines by the bed and nibbling on a few before rising helped tremendously. Occasionally a smell would strike her as odd and suddenly bring on a wave on nausea. One evening Carol was cooking supper and called me for help; the sight of eggs scrambling in the pan was suddenly revolting to her. She ran for the bathroom as I took over at the stove.

Some women seem especially subject to mood swings during pregnancy; Carol was one of them. Everyday occurrences would inexplicably be funny to her, and at other times everything seemed terribly sad and brought tears to her eyes. But she didn't see any of this as unusual. She would defend herself strongly stating undeniably that she was NOT moody.

Nathan was born in February of 1980, so when we took our vacation to Garden City Beach in September of 1979 she was hardly showing. We did all the usual things people do at the beach - walk the grand strand, swim in the ocean, lay in the sun to tan, and of course, build a sandcastle.

But our week of fun and sun was drawing to a close; we both had to return to work the following day. Checkout for the room was 11:00 am. I had tried several times to wake my sweetheart so we could pack up the car, but she stubbornly insisted on more sleep.

At long last she sat up. "Well, before we leave I want a nice breakfast. I saw a terrific buffet at one of the hotels down the road." I readily agreed, just glad to finally get her moving.

We drove up and down the long row of hotels for nearly an hour before she finally selected a restaurant; we had passed it several times, but Carol would never admit that she couldn't remember the name of the correct hotel. Inside we enjoyed a nice breakfast with all the trimmings, but I sensed she was stalling - doing her best to keep from leaving the lazy beach to return to the humdrum of work.

Returning to our little motel, I was starting to pack the car when she produced another delay tactic. In her sweetest voice and eyes like Scarlett O'Hara she pleaded, "Honey, I DO want to walk on the beach one more time before we leave." I looked at my watch, thinking of both the checkout time and the drive back home. I reluctantly agreed.

The sun was shining so bright, and the light reflected on every wave. I squinted against the glare and my sunburn gave mild complaints as we walked towards the sun. Soon Carol removed her sandals and walked in the edge of the ocean. Although she was wearing jeans, before long she was in the water up to her waist. Finally, the walk was complete and we trudged back toward the motel.

Inside the room I expected her to change out of the wet clothes, but she threw me another curve. "I might as well take a dip in the pool to get all this salt off me," she explained as she pulled on her swimsuit. I remained comfortable in my dry, salt-free jeans and sat by the pool as she dived, and swam, and floated.

We were getting close to the checkout time and I did NOT want to pay a late fee. She became huffy when I insisted it was time to get out of the pool so we could pack up to leave. All through the loading she hardly spoke to me. "HERE," she would say, shoving me a bag or another item. The protruding jaw and that stare said a lot more. I ignored it all, blaming it on fluctuating hormones.

At long last every item was in place, the room was empty, and we had checked out in time. She took the passenger side and sulked as I turned onto the highway.

There were two exits just a few miles apart which would lead to the main highway home. I paused at the first, but traffic prevented me from making the left turn. Carol snapped that I should go on down to the next exit. I let it roll off my back; I saw the moodiness and didn't let it bother me. I drove on to the second exit.

The second exit was just as crowded as the first, and I waited to make the left turn. Carol snapped again, "If you had taken the first turn, we'd be 20 miles down the road by now." I gave her a sideways glance, but I said nothing.

Finally the traffic eased and I turned onto the highway. It would be smooth sailing from here. Just four hours and we could settle back down into a normal routine. Maybe Carol would nap during the ride.

But something was wrong. Carol sat there, glaring at me with her arms crossed. Obviously I had offended her in some way. "What's wrong?" I asked.

Carol took a deep breath before she explained. "I see you put the sun on MY side of the car again!"

My jaw dropped in disbelief. All these delay tactics this morning, anything and everything to prevent us from leaving, and now I am responsible for what direction the sun rises?

It was too much. I burst out laughing. She was still mad and glowering at me. I was laughing so hard that I had to pull over to the side of the road. Finally she, too, saw that it WAS rather ridiculous to blame me for the direction the sun rose, and she laughed, too.

That little event became a benchmark with us. Years later, if I found her unhappy about something and unwilling to talk to me, I would ask, "Did I put the sun on your side of the car again, Honey?"

I'm Going to Give you a House

Carol and I were enjoying an evening stroll after supper, wandering down this street and that. On the right we approached a two-story white house; ivy was climbing up the sides. Carol didn't notice the for sale sign in the yard.

"What do you think of this one, Honey? Do you like it?" I asked as we stood in front.

Carol wrinkled up her nose. "No, it's ugly. It looks like a box."

We had gone walking almost every evening for two weeks. Each time we chose a different direction. Time and again I asked what she liked and disliked about various homes. Carol was suspicious, but I was still evading her questions.

I noticed a gray stone house of the left; it appeared to be vacant. When I asked her about this one, she suddenly turned and faced me. "Alright now, Barry Holcomb. This has been going on long enough. What are you up to?" she asked with fists poised defiantly on her hips.

I looked in her eyes and then looked away. How could I explain this without sounding ridiculous? "I am trying to find us a house" I answered gently. I knew it didn't make sense. We were barely able to pay our rent and utilities. We had no savings, nothing for a down payment.

We continued walking as we talked. I agreed that I didn't see how we could buy a house, but I wanted to keep on looking. I was learning about her tastes and what appealed to her in houses. I had even been reading the classifieds and made several calls about prices, down payments, and loan requirements. Real estate was new to me.

Carol was trying to discourage me. Although the walks were interesting she saw it as a fruitless effort at this point in our lives. She couldn't understand why I wanted to continue searching.

There was no way around it; I had to explain to her my reasons for looking. "Honey, you know I get up and have my devotions every morning."

Carol nodded her head. Now I feared I was going to sound off my rocker. "Well, last week I 'heard' something."

Carol stopped in her tracks. She asked me what I "heard." I explained that I was praying and the words "I am going to give you a house" came to my mind.

I thought I had been distracted. I dismissed the thought and continued to pray. The words came back, stronger. I stood up, got a drink of water and tried to clear my mind. "Surely I am imagining this," I thought to myself. I tried to return to my list of requests for people sick or needing work.

But the words kept coming back, stronger each time. I started talking out loud. "Lord, this doesn't make sense. Forgive me, I don't mean to make things up." I continued protesting that I didn't have the funds or the income to buy a house. But the words kept returning, each time a little stronger.

Finally the words came so forcefully they seemed almost audible. "I SAID I am going to give you a house. Why won't you believe Me?"

That got my attention. I didn't want to disbelieve. But it didn't make sense to me. I gave in. "OK, Lord. I sure want a house. I don't know how it will happen. I'll try not to doubt You." Suddenly the pressure was gone. I stood up, not knowing how to proceed.

That day I bought a paper and began reading the ads. I started learning a little about real estate. Now I was trying to find out what I should be looking for.

Carol had listened to all of this without saying a word. We turned and started walking again. Was she going to think I am crazy? Neither of us spoke for several minutes.

Finally Carol broke the ice. "Well, if God is going to give us a house, tell Him I want one with a shower. I am sick of that humongous bathtub." We both burst into laughter. I was so relieved that she didn't think I had slipped off my rocker. We agreed that we wanted to believe but found it difficult. Carol said she would help me look as we took a "wait and see" approach.

Soon our concept of the little dream house began to take shape. Carol wanted a one-story house. In the tiny apartment she had to climb the stairs every time she needed to use the bathroom. I preferred a brick home, fearing termites in a wooden structure. I also thought a carport would be an excellent addition to eliminate scraping frost and ice from the windshield on wintry mornings. And I began to take practical steps as well, applying with Farmer's Home Administration to qualify for a first time buyer's loan.

Carol and I continued our search for the house, but we kept that Voice I had heard to ourselves. Soon we had a genuine reason to search for a house; Carol was pregnant. We were giddy with excitement to be expecting our first child, but now I felt an urgency to find the dream house. The tiny apartment would rapidly become crowded with an infant in the family.

Carol and I dreamed of what we hoped our first house would be like. It became a private joke between us, but Carol would say, "When you talk to God, tell Him I need this added to the list." And it had actually become a list of details we hoped to find in the dream house. We were looking for a one-story house, brick, with a carport, and a shower. I had added that I wanted a chain-link fence around a yard big enough for a child to play in. I hoped for room for a garden and a utility shed to hold the tools. With a baby on the way, Carol suggested we ask for a washer and dryer to handle the extra laundry we would have. I didn't like the electric range of the apartment and wanted a gas range. I hoped we would have three bedrooms - a master bedroom, a nursery, and a guest room.

As I became more experienced in searching for real estate, the practical details took shape as well. FHA approved us for a loan as long as we closed the deal within six months. The required down payment was small, and my father gave it to us. Now, we just had to find that house.

Carol was getting heavy by this time, and touring homes wasn't so easy anymore. At home, she despaired of going up and down the stairs frequently to use the bathroom. Together we visited a variety of houses; most of them were out of the price range FHA had approved. But even when they weren't, they just didn't "feel" right.

At work my radar zeroed in on the words "vacant house" from a friend's conversation; on a hunch, I asked her the location of the mystery house. I drove past it on the way home from work that day. There was no "for sale" sign in the yard, but I seemed to feel it calling to me. I parked the car and walked around the lot.

It was a one-story brick house. It had a carport. I peeped in through the windows; it was furnished, but there was no sign anyone was living there. On tiptoe I could see a kitchen with a gas range, a dining room, a living room, and three small bedrooms. Inside the carport was a utility room with a washer and dryer. The house sat on a nice flat yard, and a chain-link fence surrounded the back. Even the utility shed was there.

I was flabbergasted. Every detail on the list was there. I rushed home and met Carol at the door. "Get in the car," I urged. "You've got to come see this." I pulled into the driveway and stopped. She sat frozen, almost afraid to exit the car.

I helped her stand, and together we walked around the lot. Carol began counting off the details, listing everything we had hoped to find. The bathroom window was a little higher than the others. We found a crate and I stood on it to peer inside. "Does it have a shower? Does it have a shower?" Carol asked with excitement.

The sun was going down and the shadows made it difficult to see. "Well, does it?" she asked again. As I turned, she was puzzled by my expression.

"Yeah," I drawled, "but it's purple."

Carol insisted I must be mistaken. I helped her balance on the crate to see for herself. Now she wore the puzzled expression. "Maybe it's blue or gray. I can't tell."

We knocked on the neighbor's door to learn more about the house. The retired minister and his wife revealed that an older couple had purchased the house five years earlier but had never moved in. The friendly folk shared with us the owner's name and address. They lived in New Jersey.

We were so excited; the entire evening the house was the only topic of discussion. Did they want to sell it? Would it be in our price range? How long would it take since they live so far away? It was already November, and the baby was due in February. I sincerely hoped we could close the deal and move in before the baby arrived.

I looked towards the ceiling, asking for wisdom before I wrote to the owners. I explained that we were a young married couple, expecting our first child, and were looking to buy a house. I stated simply that we had been praying for a house and their home looked like just the right one. I asked them to write or call and let me know if they were willing to sell the house.

In a few days I received a call from the couple in New Jersey. They were willing to sell the house; in a month or two they would come to South Carolina and meet to discuss it.

It was pins and needles for us for weeks; so much we still didn't know. We had not actually been inside the house. Carol and I returned and stood on that crate several times looking at the bathroom. We still weren't sure if it was purple or not.

At long last our wait was over. The Pellegrins came to South Carolina and we were able to tour the house. Carol made a beeline for the bathroom to look at the shower. The tub, shower, sink, tile and even the toilet were all lavender. It wasn't your everyday bathroom, but she could live with it.

The elderly Pellegrins were Jewish. They were hesitant to speak of their faith, but they respected our honesty for telling them we had prayed for a house. Perhaps that honesty was a factor in the final sale; in a deal that still baffles me today, the couple sold us the house and land for EXACTLY the same price they had paid five years earlier. A real estate agent would have pressured them to increase the price. It was worth twice the price they gave us.

We moved into our little dream house on Feb 23, 1980. Nathan was born four days later. Mary Black Hospital in Spartanburg was 40 miles away, but I gladly drove back and forth to visit my wife and my first born. But in 48 hours we had a massive snowstorm for SC – 12 inches – which curtailed my jaunting up and down the highway. When the doctor released Carol and Nathan to come home, I had to ask a friend with a 4 wheel drive to take me to Spartanburg and bring my family home.

Whenever Carol shared the story of God giving us the house and our list of details, I always made sure she mentioned the bathroom. "God has a sense of humor. You told Him you wanted a shower, but you didn't say what COLOR!"

The following cartoon appeared in newspapers on Feb 23, 1980 - the day we moved into the house with the purple bathroom. I kept the original until it became so faded and tattered that in 1985 I wrote Hank Ketcham and told him the story. He gladly mailed me a signed copy which you see reproduced here.

Cartoon used with permission by
Hank Ketchum Enterprises.

Of Gardens and Tillers

My first vegetable garden was unforgettable, not because of my over-whelming success as a horticulturist but because of how naïve I was. My wife and I moved into our first house in February and dreamed of an adorable vegetable garden in the summer. When spring arrived she selected a sunny little plot and bought a hoe, shovel, and a few hand gardening tools. At a yard sale, I snatched up a used tiller expecting to plant the entire garden the following Saturday.

I marked the plot, gassed up the tiller and yanked the cord. The sputter and the thrum of the engine brought back memories of my dad working his garden. Countless times I had seen him guide the tiller, churning up the earth. And oh how many vegetables came out of his garden year after year. This was going to be easy, or so I thought.

I shifted the tiller into gear and the machine lunged forward, yanking me back and forth behind it like a rag doll. At the end of the row I turned to look at the results. Behind me, the row was virtually untouched. A little bit of grass was pressed down - nothing more.

I turned the monster machine around, securing the drag to force the tiller to dig downward rather than dance across the surface. Once in gear, the tiller fought to break the hard red clay. I must be making progress I thought. Grass was flying everywhere, and the churning of the tines created a red dust cloud visible for two miles. I was certain it must have dug a foot at least; putting the machine in neutral, I pulled it back. The tiller had jerked, churned and bounced for five minutes, and the tines had only dug an inch at the most.

My equally naïve wife eased up beside me, sporting a cute little straw hat and gardening gloves, and carrying a tray of seedlings. "When can I plant these?" she asked, trying to smile through the obvious disappointment at not finding nice smooth furrows.

I attempted to break the ground with a shovel, forcing the blade a couple of inches into the soil. But when I pulled back, the handle snapped off in my hands. This ground had been unbroken for at least twenty years, maybe much longer.

The only tool capable of breaking the soil was a pick. It took me two days to break up the plot with the pick and then several more tilling it time and again to break the boulders of red clay down to a workable size.

That first year, the yield was pitiful. The plants tried in vain to suck any life from the red gravel masquerading as earth. The plants were peaked and spindly, the fruit small and thin. The entire summer we struggled with the garden, getting disappointing results.

I consulted several gardening magazines and built a compost bin, filling it with every leaf and grass clipping, as well as vegetable scraps from the kitchen. The following spring I had a rich black supplement to enrich and loosen my soil.

That year I could break up the clay with the tiller. Vermiculite, peat moss, cow manure, and the rich mixture from my compost bin were all blended into the orange soil. We grew tomatoes that were actually red rather than a pale pink, and the beans produced generously, not just a few pods per plant. The squash were round and plump, no longer spindly.

Each year I added compost and manure, increasing the nutrients in the ground. Coffee grounds, egg shells, and apple peels all contributed to the mulch. Each year the ground was easier to break and the yield more plentiful. We bought a chest freezer to preserve the harvest; we still enjoyed our delicious vegetables into the following year. After five years, the ground was no longer red clay - it was a rich black soil. When spring arrived, I turned the ground easily with just a spade. And the rich black earth made all the vegetables grow plump and beautiful.

Maybe you already know where this object lesson is going. We are called to break up the fallow ground of our hearts, the ground which has become baked and hardened by disuse. Do I have a hardened heart? Does God have difficulty breaking the ground of my soul to implant the seed of inspiration?

When we face hardship and trials, is God knocking on the door of our heart? It is our choice how to respond when problems arise. We can be hard and stubborn, wondering with anger why adversity has arisen, or we can look above, seeing if He desires a change in our attitudes, our hearts, or our direction. The same sunshine which bakes the brick also opens the crocus and the daffodil.

Touch of a Loving Hand

The atmosphere was thick with tension. "Daddy, I want to go home," my three-year-old son pleaded.

I held his hand and explained it just once more: "Nathan, the doctor says you've got to stay here in the hospital until you get better." His little green eyes implored me to carry him away.

It was only early afternoon, but I felt as though a year had passed in the eight hours since we had been here. He had been vomiting for three days and now was badly dehydrated. The doctor suspected it was only a virus; here Nathan could receive an IV to replace the lost fluids, and close monitoring would reveal if his illness was more serious.

But inserting that IV had not been easy. That morning the nurse had been as gentle as she could. But the small veins of a child, shrunk further by dehydration, made her task more difficult. We had explained it to Nathan, and even though he didn't understand, he didn't resist.

He bit his lower lip and looked away as she probed the veins in one hand unsuccessfully. He was holding onto his bravery as best he could. The nurse remained calm and moved to try a vein in the other hand. Her touch was gentle, but his weariness made the stick of the tiny needle seem much greater. His lip started to quiver. He gave a low moan as a tear ran down one cheek.

The nurse apologized to my wife and myself. "I'm so sorry. I don't want to frighten him. I'm paging the nurse from pediatrics; she has more experience with tiny veins than I do."

In a few minutes another nurse was standing at the foot of the bed. In an instant she saw our son's fear and our worry. She gently asked us to wait in the hallway, explaining that he would remain calm if he didn't see our worried eyes watching her every move.

We told Nathan we would be right back and not to worry. We put on phony smiles as we trudged out the door. But just as soon as we were out the door, we turned and opened it just enough to peek. "What do you see? Is he alright?" We both stood on tiptoe, taking turns pressing our noses to the crack to watch our brave son.

In just seconds the nurse opened the door, and we rushed back to the bedside. The IV was in one hand, and there were no tears on his face. When we turned to thank the nurse, she was already gone.

Nathan was quiet now, but drained. He still wanted to be in his own bed. My wife and I were exhausted, more from the stress than physical weariness. Nathan was trying to cooperate, but he just could not understand how this needle in his hand could make him well.

He was weak and worn out. If he could only rest, the IV would replenish his fluids and strength. Despite all our attempts, he would not lie still and go to sleep. As we worried, despair began to creep into our thoughts. The four walls were closing in as the atmosphere grew thicker with the anxiety.

And then a gentle tap sounded at the door. His day-care teacher, Helein Rogers, had come to learn what was wrong. As she whispered her questions, we saw the genuine concern on her face. Somehow she shared our load and decreased our burden.

And then she went to his bedside. "Nathan, tell me about the doctor." From his fragments and nervous stammerings, she pieced together his worries. He showed her the IV in his hand and the matching bandage on his teddy's arm.

Miss Helein looked into his eyes and held his undivided attention. "Nathan, your Mommy and Daddy tell me that you need a nap."

"I want to go home," he complained. "I don't want to take a nap."

In some miraculous way she received his objection and transformed it with a few gentle words. "Nathan, your head is saying 'I don't want to take a nap' but your body is saying something else. It's saying, 'I'm so tired. Please let me sleep. I would feel so much better.'"

Nathan listened to every word. Already I could see the furrows leaving his little brow. Somehow the words affected me as well. The knots in my shoulders began to melt.

"Turn over on your side," Miss Helein directed. "Now, put your hand over your eyes just like at naptime. Now close the cracks." He had been so tired but too anxious to relax. In seconds his breathing changed as he drifted off in soft slumber. Everything was under control again.

If this kindness were not enough, Miss Helein brought his favorite storybook and some pictures to color. Words alone could not express our thanks. She quietly left, asking us to call her later.

The IV did its work, and overnight Nathan's strength returned; the following morning the doctor released him to return home.

That day in the hospital seemed much longer than it really was, and even though the procedures were simple, they were frightening to a small child who only wanted to go home. Three years later I still remember with gratitude the kindness and thoughtfulness of a not-so-ordinary daycare worker.

It's a Girl

I clutch my wife's hand lying limp at her side. The anesthetist applies the oxygen mask. The doctor is just getting into position. In his mask and cap I recognize him only by his voice. The nurse moves about the delivery room in final preparations for the new arrival. A long day of pain and endurance is almost complete.

"Now, PUSH" the doctor tells her. Even under heavy sedation Carol responds to his direction. In seconds the head emerges. My pulse is pounding, and I grip the edge of the table in anticipation. The doctor cleans the nostrils and mouth with the ease of experience. "Push again," he says, and into his massive hands he receives my daughter, lifting her high for me to see.

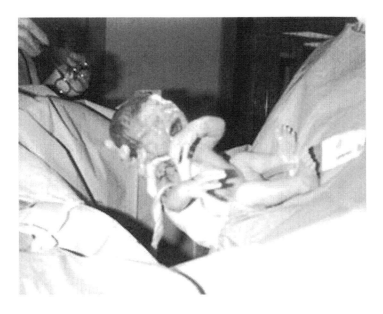

As I look upon this tiny life, my eyes begin to well up with tears. I am awed by the love of a woman willing and happy to endure this for me. Already my arms ache to hold my daughter's tiny heart close to mine. My mind has left the delivery room, already thinking of her needs tomorrow and in years to come. The responsibility is welcome to these shoulders.

Back in delivery, Carol is fighting to come our of the haze. "What did we have?" she whispers. On hearing my answer, she too has teary eyes. From deep within, a new strength rises through the exhaustion. "I want to hold her."

Again my emotions are rolling. In spite of all our failures and selfishness, God gives us so many lessons about Himself. If we as mere human parents can give so much of ourselves and can love so deeply, how much more does our Creator love us! His love is too great for any finite mind to hold. How is it possible to disbelieve?

The effects of the anesthesia still linger. Carol asks me again. I take her hand in mine again. "It's a girl, Sweetheart. It's a girl!"

Well, What do you Expect?

Sunday mornings were often hectic at our little home on Sunset Boulevard; aside from the normal getting ourselves bathed and dressed, we had two little ones to serve breakfast and dress before we left for church. I frequently said, "Forget trying to arrive on TIME. Just GETTING to church with two little ones is an accomplishment."

And this morning had been just that kind of morning - changing diapers, washing faces and wiping runny noses and trying to keep ourselves looking presentable at the same time. Finally, we had the children safely placed in the nursery and we sat down only a few minutes late in Sunday School.

This morning the teacher read the familiar creation story from Genesis including the creation of Eve from Adam's rib. The speaker looked at all of us and concluded, "Every living thing, including Adam was made from the dust of the earth, but Eve was made from Adam's rib and was the only living thing NOT made from the earth. Do you suppose this could account for some of the differences we typically see between the two genders?"

Carol was really enjoying the discussion as each person made a comment on qualities they thought are typically masculine and feminine. Suddenly, she too had an idea and made a comment. "Women are usually more sentimental and remember things like birthdays and important dates, but men often don't."

The entire back row burst into laughter as they heard my grumbling response, "What what do you expect? I'm only made out of MUD!"

Lordy, Lordy, I Don't Want to be Forty

Carol had returned to work from disability and was doing fairly well, but I noticed something was bothering her. She and I often talked about her therapy; she looked to me for support and encouragement, often feeling that nothing was changing. She often discussed her assignments with me.

"How did you feel when you turned 40?" she asked one day. I had passed that hurdle two years earlier. Her nervousness tipped me that her upcoming birthday was a source of anxiety.

"It bothered me a little," I admitted, "but it certainly wasn't a mid-life crisis." I shared that I became introspective for a month or so; I looked back not with regrets but with a certain amount of disappointment. So many dreams had just withered away as impractical. The twinges I felt were a mild sadness that I had not accomplished more in my 40 years.

Carol's expression told me she was absorbing all my words. Finally she admitted that she was dreading what might happen at work. "Honey, you don't know how horrible they treat some ladies on their 40th birthday." Carol went on to explain; "In one office they gave a secretary a tombstone cake. In another one they gave the receptionist a big bouquet of dead roses, delivered by a man in a hearse." Carol told stories of offices decorated with black balloons and over-the-hill banners; the ladies laughed at their gifts. But some of them went to the bathroom so no one would see them cry.

I hugged her, assuring her that I didn't think her office would do anything like that. At the same time, my mind started grinding its gears. I knew I had to do something special for this birthday, something that would completely erase her fears of being over-the-hill.

Fortunately her birthday was several months away. What I really wanted to do was throw a big surprise party and invite college friends and relatives to come. But everyone was so scattered out. Some friends were in Colorado. Aunts and Uncles were in Illinois, Georgia, and Florida. Even with this amount of time, it was an awful lot to ask them to come so far for a birthday party.

Finally, my ideas began to take shape. We had some friends at church who would help me with a surprise party, especially when I told them what was worrying her. I decided to call every friend and relative that I could find. I copied names and phone numbers out of her address book and called every one.

"I am planning a THIS IS YOUR LIFE party for Carol's 40th birthday," I told them. "I want you to think of something funny that happened between you. I will call you back tomorrow and record the story."

Balancing work and recording phone calls was quite a challenge, but from the first call I knew it would work. The person would begin by saying, "Hi, Carol. I remember when . . . " Each person told of an event, not revealing who he or she was; at the end the caller would identify himself and wish her Happy Birthday.

When I began the task of editing the tape, I had quite a collection of messages. It wasn't just going to work; it was going to be GREAT!

Carol's Sunday school class helped wonderfully. The teacher called and asked Carol to come and help her review new curriculum for the children's classes. We planned the party a day before her birthday to keep her from getting suspicious. She believed I had to work that night.

That afternoon I raced all around Charlotte, picking up the kids and the cake and sneaking into the house just moments before she arrived. At the shout of "Surprise!" I knew I had succeeded. That beaming smile showed no sign of worry, just sheer joy at being remembered.

Her friends greeted her with hugs and kisses. Her laughs and tears flowed freely. The ladies presented her with homemade cards bearing messages of fads from years gone by.

As master of ceremonies I introduced the This Is Your Life program. We placed her in the hot seat and started the tape; she was greeted by aunts and uncles, her mother and father, and cousins. She was amazed to hear her college roommate, her high school pastor, even her childhood piano teacher greet her and tell tales on her. And then, I gave the final message, reminding her of funny events, cooking disasters, my own blunders, and some of our wonderful times together. The program closed with a recording of our college choir singing "All Our Friends."

The happy wishes overwhelmed her heart, but on the refreshment table was the *pi'ece de r'esistance*. A small wind-up train chugged away atop the cake. The icing message read "I love you Train-loads."

Carol later called many of her recorded well-wishers, telling them about the party and how she appreciated their messages. It brought back so many happy memories. She listened to the tape many times.

I look back on that party as one of the greatest things I have ever done. I managed to take an event she was dreading and change it into one of her happiest memories.

The Broken Camera

Sometimes God speaks in little whispers, and other times His voice is so clear it's impossible to mistake the message or the Speaker. One time He moved and spoke in a remarkable way, in a Kodak moment that brought me from despair to wonder. It has made a tremendous difference in how I have perceived things since then.

I stood by a pile of clutter on the living room floor, about to drop the broken camera in my hand onto it. Surely I had no use for this piece of junk, but I just couldn't let it go.

It had been a difficult four months since my wife passed away. So much to do, so many decisions to make and the constant battle with raw emotions consumed me even during the basic tasks of daily life. Twenty years of marriage to a wonderful woman had suddenly ended; I knew it was coming, but some things are impossible to prepare for. Here I was - 44 years old, the father of two teenagers, suddenly finding myself a widower and a single parent.

Life had been difficult for quite some time - 10 years actually; my wife, only two years younger than myself, was always plagued by mysterious pains and ailments. Time and again doctors had treated symptoms, giving a new diagnosis and temporary relief, but after a few months a new problem would arise.

Outwardly our lives appeared normal and happy: a young married couple with two children, just like the Berenstein Bears, father, mother, son, and daughter. Carol worked as a legal secretary; her skills were phenomenal - typing at 100 wpm and a memory of every file and letter and where to find them. I worked as a restaurant manager. I was outgoing with my customers, hard-working, respected by my employees.

But if I sat quietly, I had the ominous feeling that trouble was coming. The mysterious ailments increased until Carol had to be hospitalized. The doctor ordered various tests and scans but could find no physical cause for her recurring problems. Believing her symptoms were psychosomatic, he referred us to a psychiatrist.

At first the suggestion seemed out of line. I was a bit offended. But considering it slowly and carefully, I could see perhaps repressed problems were plaguing my wife. I began to see reason in his referral.

But still, we were regular churchgoers. We had blessings at mealtime and I arose to read my Bible and pray every morning. We had little prayer times with the kids most nights. Carol even played the organ and piano at church. Why was this happening to us?

The psychiatrist met with my wife alone briefly and then with both of us at length. She began sessions with a therapist to help her deal with the emotional issues she was battling. The psychiatrist would see her occasionally to review her progress and to alter prescriptions as needed.

Initially I found it depressing to admit this problem but once I did, it gave a glimmer of hope that longstanding issues could actually be resolved. It would be too long and sad a story to go into all the details - sickness, depression, anxiety, panic attacks, phobias and compulsions, repeated hospitalizations, hopes built up and knocked down over and over again. And more and more trips to doctor after doctor - and hospitalizations time and again. We came to know every emergency room and psychiatric ward in the city.

I didn't find it difficult to be both mama and daddy to the kids, at least not at first. I was handy in the kitchen. I knew how to do laundry and to shop. It was the long hours that wore me down; between 60-hour work weeks and caring for the kids and housework, my strength diminished. My cheerfulness faded. I plodded to and from work.

Still I held on. I took the kids to church alone when Carol was too ill to come with us. I tried to cook those special things that would make her smile. I never told her how things were going at work; she was distressed enough. She didn't need to hear that I wasn't coping with my tasks well. The demotion was something I would keep secret from her for a long time.

I had to plan ahead for Christmas to stretch every penny so all of us had at least one special thing. I started months ahead, buying little things for the kids and for the stockings, squirreling them away. I noticed how her hand lingered over that bracelet at the jewelry counter; she withdrew and looked away, never telling me how she longed for it. I went back the next day and put down a deposit. She would find it under the tree Christmas morning.

Sometimes it was just a little thing. Maybe we couldn't really afford it, but I would find a way. "Honey, get dressed. I want to take you somewhere." It took such an effort for her to come out of the house; she smiled nervously as we sat in the quaint coffee shop I had found. Although just a tiny place, they served soup and fresh bread. They even baked cookies and brought them hot from the oven. She had little appetite, but the aromas and the surroundings cheered her.

Some families experience turmoil as their kids pass through the teen years; our time was pretty rocky. I think Nathan and Adria were under more anxiety than others. Their mother was never well, and she was often irritable because of her pain. And their Dad was always working. I believe they had a pretty rough time of it.

Nathan performed poorly in high school. Although he had no lack of intelligence, he had no interest. I had been to the principal's office repeatedly trying to find a combination that worked. But dropping and adding classes and changing schedules did no good. He was absolutely miserable. Now not only was he failing every subject, but he had skipped so many days that I was in danger of legal action. If he missed any more days I would have to appear before court and face a fine or maybe even jail time.

I refused to allow Nathan to drop out of school with no education and no job skills. So I gave him the choice of immediately going to work fulltime or signing up for Job Corps where he could receive both job training AND education. It was a difficult transition attending Job Corps, but he showed his ability, completing his GED in just two weeks. When he was given the opportunity to enlist in the Army, I thought maybe he had finally found his niche. He joined and the structure seemed very good for him.

Adria, too, struggled with my wife's illness. My son's absence made the house empty, and the conflict between mother and daughter was intensified. Carol wanted to be with her daughter, but found herself irritated easily. Adria couldn't understand her illness and anxiety and wanted to be with friends instead.

Then problems developed with my son in the Army. He had terrible back pain that would not respond to treatment. After two months in the infirmary, they made a diagnosis of scoliosis and issued a medical discharge. I questioned God again. Why did He lead me to believe we had found the proper path for him, only to snatch it away? The reason for his return home would appear sooner than I expected.

The battles with depression were now over. Carol had chosen to end her life quietly while everyone else was out of the house. Nathan had returned only a week before. It was he who found her and called me. I heard the pain in his voice; I knew what had happened even before he told me. I rushed home, my eyes blurred with tears. The kids clung to me for what seemed an hour before I called the authorities. The next couple of hours seemed to last much longer, but the officers and the paramedics were courteous, professional, and sympathetic.

Now, the years of struggling were over - the pain, the agony, the hurt. We were putting the house up for sale. I needed to find a smaller more affordable place for the three of us. I was sorting through so many belongings, some to throw away, some to give away, some for a yard sale. Inside a cabinet I discovered the old broken camera; I stood turning it over in my hands time and again, finally dropping it onto the pile of clutter on the floor.

As I went back and forth, selecting and sorting, my thoughts kept returning to the useless camera. The last time I had taken any pictures with it, they were overexposed and ruined, but I couldn't remember how long ago that had been. I picked it up and looked at it. There was a roll of film in it, partially used. I dropped it to the floor again.

"Whatever those pictures are, they are ruined" I told myself. But as I continued to sift through papers and clutter, that camera kept pressing in on my mind. What on earth I had taken pictures of? Walking out to the dumpster, I snatched the camera back out of the trash.

The next day's mail included a developing coupon. I would use it and solve the mystery. If the photos were useless, I would discard them and not be charged. But a hunch kept telling me the camera held something worth keeping.

When I returned to collect my pictures, the clerk turned away as I opened the envelope. At once I knew God had guided my hand, stopping me from tossing the camera.

The first picture was of Nathan, some three years previous, during our vacation to Washington DC. He was so happy in the photo, before his school problems had begun.

The second was of Adria, beaming as she threw peanuts to the squirrels outside the Smithsonian. And there was a snapshot of Carol and Adria at the top floor of the Washington Monument.

All the pictures were perfect. And then, I pulled out the most special photo of all. My mouth fell open, and my eyes filled with tears. There were all four of us, hugging and smiling in front of the Capitol. I had no memory of asking someone to take the picture. Completely absorbed in the photos, I stood there for several minutes as the memories flooded over me.

Carol had been in a period of remission; the depression was gone and she was like her old self again. Her therapist was seeing her less and less, and we thought she would be returning to work. I withdrew a precious little bit of savings to take us all on a trip. It was the most wonderful time we had ever shared, our happiest vacation. And it was the last time all four of us traveled together and had such a carefree time. In the sickness and pain that followed, I had completely forgotten that week.

The mysterious camera had yielded a priceless treasure. Why had I used a camera that I knew was defective? Why had the broken camera worked this one time? Why had I never developed the film? How had the camera been misplaced for three years? And thankfully, now God had stopped me from throwing the camera away.

Time has passed now; we have a smaller house. Nathan is out on his own, working well at a restaurant. Adria is leaving for college in a few days. The black times are only a blurry memory. But hanging on the wall are treasured photos of a trip to Washington, with the wife and mother we loved and remember, beautiful evidence of God's hand guiding even when we don't recognize it.

The Camel's Final Journey

It was my first Christmas as a widower. After 20 years of holiday traditions wrapped up in my wife and children, I was facing my first holiday as a single parent.

I opened up the Christmas decorations slowly. I am deeply sentimental and every ornament had memories attached to it. What was I going to do with the ceramic nativity set? We had used it every year since my son was born. I had molded and fired the entire set, and Carol had meticulously painted each piece. For 18 years, the nativity set had been the first Christmas decoration to unpack, and until January 1, it would be the center of attention.

Perhaps my pain was more intense this first Christmas without her, but every time I looked at it I could see Carol holding and carefully painting each piece. I felt I could not bear such tangible reminders of her the entire Christmas season. But what would I do with the precious set? I had no desire to destroy it, but I didn't want just to give the entire set away, either. I was considering not mailing any Christmas cards this year when an idea dawned on me; in just a few moments I knew EXACTLY what I would do.

From my address book, I selected names of near and dear family and friends. At work the next day, I searched for boxes of varied sizes; that night I set my plan into motion.

Opening the large box of shredded paper, I carefully placed each figure on the kitchen table. I placed Mary, Joseph, and Baby Jesus in the center and around them all the other pieces: three wise men, three shepherds, an angel, a cow, a donkey, and three camels. All but one I rewrapped and packed in separate boxes. But the Baby in the manger was not wrapped. He was staying here with me.

I wrote a little note to each person, explaining the history of the nativity set. "The nativity set is so wrapped up with memories that I can no longer use it, but I thought since Carol was special to you that you might like one piece as a memento."

Most pieces I randomly matched with a name of a friend or relative.

I chose pieces to ship to a college professor, a music teacher, a pastor, a college roommate, a cousin. But one piece was different: the standing camel, the largest of all the pieces I felt should go to Carol's Aunt Helen in Florida. I had heard she suffered from terminal cancer.

Aunt Helen had always held a special place in our hearts. We had spent one Christmas with her in Atlanta. She was so childlike herself;

we all laughed while Nathan sat on her lap for 45 minutes, giggling, wiggling and squirming as she pretended to cut his hair. We remembered her high-pitched laugh and her unending repertoire of light-hearted stories.

Some years earlier Helen had undergone surgery and radiation treatments for endometrial cancer. Recently the doctors had discovered that the cancer had returned and metastasized to her lungs. It was so wide-spread that surgery was impossible.

The next day I stood in a long line at the post office, both arms full with packages. If I accomplished nothing else today, the camel had to be mailed.

When he arrived in Florida, Aunt Helen was in the hospital with severe complications; he was taken to her room and placed on her bedside table amid get well and Christmas cards. She didn't say much, but Helen was very touched to be remembered in a tangible way. Carol had been a special niece to her, and it meant a great deal to have a physical remembrance, something she had made, used and treasured.

The doctors had already revealed to Helen that her time was limited. They could only attempt to make her comfortable. Helen was discharged from the hospital to spend Christmas at home. Her own nativity set was on a table in the family room, and the special camel stood on the hearth by the fireplace. He kept a watchful eye over Helen as she moved about the house during the holidays.

Shortly after Christmas, Helen fell to the floor. She claimed to be fine, but when her breathing was labored, her daughter Karen took her to the emergency room, where the examining physician discovered a collapsed lung. She was re-admitted to the hospital for a matter of days, before hospice came to offer assistance.

Helen returned home after a short while, and the Christmas tree and decorations were soon packed away. But the camel kept his appointed post on the hearth, overseeing the family room, searching for the star, and watching over Helen.

Perhaps she noticed the camel often; maybe Helen was quiet because she was so weak. Several rounds of chemotherapy had given her a little bit of improvement, but they had also taken a heavy toll on her strength. Helen had always been a cheerful person, easy to laugh and quick to encourage. But years of battling with cancer, the exhaustion of chemotherapy, and the discouragements of one setback after another had robbed her of much of that cheerfulness.

After Christmas, in spite of more difficulties, friends and family noticed a little of her old self returning. Maybe it was the Christmas season; maybe it was the cards and the well wishes. Or just maybe Helen was watching for the natal star, too.

The camel stayed close by, never packed away, continually watching as Helen continued her battle against cancer. On March 25, 1999, with her daughter, her sister, and her best friend holding her hands, Helen closed her eyes. She had found the star and stepped from this world into the light. Her journey was ended.

The camel still remains in Florida in the home of another relative. Norma, well known for her generosity and Christmas spirit, enjoys the company of the camel who reminds her of Helen and of Carol. The camel encourages her as well on her search for the natal star.

The Final Impression

Without a doubt, she was a difficult customer. No matter how I tried, she had one complaint after another. My first instinct was to reflect her attitude, but I had a hunch there was more here than met the eye. Perhaps this middle-aged, heavy-set woman had faced one problem after another and not heard a kind word the entire day. I resolved to serve her as though she were my own mother.

Why would I take the trouble to be kind to someone I might never see again? A few years ago I developed the attitude of giving people a good FINAL impression rather than a special FIRST impression. Here is the reason.

My wife had not been well for quite some time. She was suffering from clinical depression and was struggling to pull herself back together again.

Once before she had been disabled for nearly three years; somehow with the help of therapists, psychiatrists, medications, and prayers she crept out of the darkness. She struggled to regain job skills after computers had revolutionized the word processing field. We had no computer at home, but in a few months she learned various computer systems, Word, Lotus, spreadsheets and filing systems. Daily she went to the employment agency, studying manuals and performing tutorials to master the new technology. She even checked out instructional materials from the public library and tested tricks and techniques on the agency computer, completely amazing the instructor with her understanding and incorporating of varied systems.

It took tremendous bravery to re-enter the job force after being disabled so long. Yet somehow she did, and gained skills, speed, and friends along the way. She worked side by side with three other ladies in the legal firm's typing pool. For months they worked together, chatted about their families, and helped one another time and again.

For nearly two years her work performance was amazing. She rapidly adapted to changes in the computer system which frustrated the entire firm. She even constructed an in-house manual, giving detailed instructions to any novice on the quickest way to navigate the system, avoid pitfalls, to create documents and how to find them.

I don't know what went wrong. Perhaps her medication no longer controlled the chemical imbalance. Perhaps there was some injury she wouldn't reveal to the therapist. But I could see trouble coming.

Work started taking a toll on her; each day she was more tired than the one before. Her amazing memory and concentration lost some of their luster, and her eyes began to lose their gleam.

Eventually she was barely able to function. She made one mistake after another, lost documents, couldn't keep up with the pace, and suffered migraines and frequent ailments.

Her condition declined until she required several hospitalizations for depression. Each time she returned, better for a short period, but still not her old energetic and bright self. The law firm counseled her and warned her about her declining performance, but eventually they had little choice but to let her go.

Getting fired would be discouraging to anyone, but it is a crushing blow to someone already suffering from depression. The loss of income pushed her even farther into the darkness.

The government scrutinizes anyone who has been on disability and who after a period of recovery needs to return to state assistance. The agencies doubted the letters and forms from her doctors and insisted she see a psychiatrist of their own choosing. This doctor also questioned if her decline was genuine or just an attempt to escape from work. The sky grew even darker above her.

It was when she was so low that she thought of visiting her old friends at the word-processing pool. I encouraged her, hoping it would improve her outlook. Doubting herself the whole time, she spruced up, fixing her hair, choosing a cheerful dress, donning a shining necklace. After a nervous drive, she stood in the office where they had spent so many hours together. The three ladies said how much they missed her and were so glad to see her; they complimented her figure and asked when she was returning to work.

She said her goodbyes and left the room. Just outside the door a familiar attorney stopped her to chat. But inside the office behind her, the conversation suddenly changed. "God, did you see how BAD she looks? I can't believe she went out in a dumpy dress like that." They tore her down, from her hair now gray and stringy from medications to her weight and make-up.

In the hallway the attorney stood paralyzed and helpless. He saw the agony in her eyes and tried to apologize as she slipped out the door. She stopped several times on the way home to pull aside while she cried. She wept almost constantly several days.

I wish I could tell you that she returned the following week and told the ladies what she thought of them. I wish I could tell you that her condition changed and that she soon re-entered the work force, rubbing shoulders with nicer people and making more money.

But that isn't what happened. Her condition grew steadily worse. The migraines and depression increased. Those ladies who complimented her to her face and then stabbed her in the back never knew. No one ever called to ask how she was feeling. Carol never spoke to any of them again.

Now a phone call or a visit from one of them might not have made any difference at all, but who knows? Had someone shown her a little kindness, given her a call, or written her a little note, it would at least have changed how she thought about them. But as it turns out, the memories of that day were the final impressions she had of her former friends.

It takes so little time to say a kind word, to open a door, to write a note or make a phone call. You may never see or speak to that person again. When they remember you, what will their final impression be?

My Snowglobe on the Shelf

D o you ever wonder, "Where did that thought come from?" Some random incident or person from years ago comes to mind for no apparent reason. My memory never seems to work the way I want or need. At times, my mind is like a junk drawer, cluttered with gadgets I rarely use but will not throw away. I open the drawer looking for a potato peeler, but I find instead a pack of twist ties and a bottle opener - interesting, but completely useless at peeling potatoes.

Some memories are fiery and too easily retrieved. As soon as you hear a name, instances of conflict come to mind and your blood pressure rises as anger burns within you. I sometimes wish I could erase those memories.

Some recollections are filed incorrectly. I draw a complete blank when trying to recall an old acquaintance. No matter what others tell me, I cannot remember him. But when someone identifies the year or the job I was doing at that time, immediately the person's face comes into view.

But the most significant recollections I call snowglobe memories. The individual events were burned into my mind because of the emotional impact they held at the time. I label them snowglobe memories, because we tend to take them out from time to time, shake them up by retelling, polish them, and place them on a pedestal for others to see.

I will share with you one of my snowglobe memories. It just happens to be about the editor of the Westmoreland News based in Montross, Virginia. Lynn Norris is my sister-in-law, and although we chat or email each other often now, such was not the case five years ago. I had not seen her for nearly 10 years and spoke with her only once or twice a year. Our only connection was her sister, my wife.

When my wife passed away on April 19, 1998, I called her sister, Lynn. She didn't burst into tears but sympathized with me and gave me some very practical advice on dealing with my situation. Over the next week we spoke several times. She even helped me write the obituary.

My wife died on Sunday, and we scheduled the service the following Saturday, allowing me time to gather my wits. It also allowed relatives time to get off jobs and drive to Charlotte from Virginia, Georgia, and Florida.

On Friday evening, relatives were meeting at my home to visit, to comfort, and to share before the service the following morning. I was both apprehensive and looking forward to their arrivals. I wanted comfort, but I feared the memories and questions which would come.

I had cleaned counters and sinks and put every piece of dirty laundry behind some closed door. I was scratching my head trying to decide what I could feed the friends and family when the doorbell rang.

In came Lynn, both arms loaded; she quickly gave me a hug, a kiss, and a "let me by so I can put these things down." Instantly, Lynn had my kitchen under her control and suggested I sit down or take a short nap.

Lynn brought flowers freshly cut from her garden, homemade bread, delicious Virginia ham, crackers, cheese, sodas, and a wonderful clarity of mind. She took the burden from my shoulders for awhile, prepared sandwiches and drinks, met the relatives at the door, and put everyone at ease.

She encouraged me, introduced strangers, and made everyone welcome. For a couple of days, when I was distraught and stressed to the maximum, she made everything easier. Her kindness showed love for me and honored her sister.

I thanked her then, I think. But I could never thank her enough.

Since then, Lynn and I have kept up with each other fairly well. Sometimes we get busy and pre-occupied with our lives, and our hectic schedules make e-mails much easier than phone conversations, but we have become quite close. She is like the sister I never had, and I hope I am like the brother she never had.

Now that I have shaken the snowglobe, and shown you the beautiful picture inside, I will polish it and return it to its pedestal. I think she deserves to be on a pedestal. Memories of kindness like this need to be shown, polished, and bragged about often.

Thank you, Sweetheart

Today is New Year's Eve 2009, and my plans for this book are near completion. I have spent four months going through three decades of writings, and the tedious tasks of compiling and editing have brought many events back as if they occurred only yesterday.

Carol and I shared 20 years of marriage - and I would not trade one minute for all the gold on the planet.

We married in August of 1977 and moved into a tiny apartment near campus. I worked as Carol continued her last two years of college. Finances were rather tight; we survived mostly on scrambled eggs, pinto beans, and grits. We were close enough that Carol could ride her bike to campus. Each Wednesday evening she drove to my Mom's house and visited while doing the laundry; I stayed home and baked bread which would last until the following Wednesday.

Our first Christmas we had a tiny little tree, with a few lights, and ornaments Carol had made by blowing out eggs and embellishing the shells with glitter and rickrack. We had a few gifts under the tree and two stockings filled. Carol pleaded to open the gifts on Christmas eve, but I insisted we wait until Christmas. 12:05 AM her alarm sounded and she shook me awake. "Hey, it's Christmas! Can we open our presents NOW?" I had no choice but to agree; we raced downstairs and opened everything like we were youngsters. She laughed and giggled over the dimestore trinkets and the bolo paddle, but her eyes filled with tears at the delicate little necklace she found in the toe of her stocking.

Carol completed her degree in piano performance and worked as a legal secretary in a small office of two lawyers. We were thrilled to be expecting our first child, but fearing the apartment would be too crowded, I desperately wanted to buy a house. We found the answer to our prayers, closing the deal and moving in on February 24, 1980. Nathan was born three days later. We were so thrilled to be parents that we had another child Adria, arriving when Nathan was three years old.

Carol suffered from the mysterious illnesses even during our courtship, and they slowly increased after the children were born. During her period of disability, money was tight, and she wanted to do something special for my birthday. She knew how much I love black-berry jelly, and when she saw some blackberries growing wild, she developed a secret plan. She returned to stand in the blazing sun, wading through brambles to pick a bucket of the wild berries. It only made a few small jars, but I treasured them as the most priceless birthday gift I ever received.

One year she was struggling after her return to work from disability. Little comments she made about herself revealed her insecurities. She didn't feel lovely anymore. She doubted everything about herself. One night she asked me if I still loved her. In the drugstore the next day I noticed a clerk opening a Valentine's display. I stood and stared at the big red hearts, urging my creative juices to flow. How could I demonstrate my love to my wife in a tangible way? I resolved this would be one Valentine's Day she would never forget.

On February 1, I didn't stop to check the mailbox as usual. When Carol arrived home from work, I spoke before she climbed the steps. "Would you bring in the mail, Hon. I'll start supper." I peeked through the blinds as she opened and closed the mailbox. She shuffled through the mail as she walked and then suddenly stopped. She turned one little card over and over but didn't open it. She dropped the rest of the mail on the sofa and walked to the bedroom with the precious little card. It wasn't fancy, and the message was corny. I had created it with Print Shop. But it was addressed to "The Most Beautiful Woman on Vista Grande Circle." After a few minutes alone she reappeared, planting a big kiss on my lips as I stirred the ground beef. She never mentioned the card.

Another card arrived in the mail on February 2, addressed to "The Most Beautiful Woman in Charlotte." A different card arrived every day; on Sunday a card would mysteriously appear somewhere that she would find it. Every day the area of the beauty competition grew, from Mecklenburg County to North Carolina to the Eastern Seaboard. By February 14 the valentine was addressed to the Most Beautiful Woman in the Galaxy. That night I took her out to dinner, giving her yellow roses and candy. She kept those silly little Valentines in a box of her most precious possessions.

One December we returned to Presbyterian College to attend the 25th Annual Madrigal Dinner. It was just as glorious as we had remembered it; Carol had been a madrigal performer all four years of college. The director invited former singers to come and vocally assist the current troupe. I was amazed how many men and women stood and joined the new singers; Carol absolutely beamed as she sang. Whenever she comes to mind, I see her wearing that gorgeous red dress.

Stirring up so many memories, happy and difficult times, put a different perspective on Christmas this year. Carol went on to her heavenly reward over 10 years ago, but this year I could almost feel her standing beside me. She watched as I hung the last surviving eggshell ornament. She approved as I arranged the nativity set, very similar to the one she painted, but which I had made and given to her parents. I felt her hovering nearby, proud of the handsome, respectful man Nathan has become. I could almost smell her perfume near me as we watched Adria on the floor helping Giovany open his gifts. Did I just imagine her standing beside the table as Michael sat with us, enjoying the Hungarian Potroast she taught me to cook? I feel her approval often as I care for him as I used to care for her.

Thank you, Sweetheart, for being my better half. You always brought out the best in me. Thank you for giving me two beautiful children. Thank you for your love, your encouragement, your trust, for doing everything you could for me. I look forward to seeing you again, released from the burdens and the illnesses you suffered on this side. I know you are waiting for me. I'm coming.

CHAPTER 2

Finding Faith

When Will Christmas Come Again?

It's been so long - I hope Christmas will come again this year. Oh, I know December 25th comes every year, but it isn't Christmas.

Maybe it was the year we bought the artificial tree. It's so easy to put up, and there are no needles to vacuum for a month. But it just hasn't been Christmas since we bought it. Or maybe it was when we had the Christmas cards printed; it's so much easier than writing all those addresses.

A few years ago I was sure that Christmas would come. I very carefully bought everyone exactly what they wanted. I called all the stores and ordered the gifts with my credit cards. They even delivered! It was so convenient; I didn't have to scrimp and save for so long. I didn't have to carry all that cash and fight through the crowds. I didn't even have to wrap anything; it was all taken care of for me.

Maybe it was the year I didn't have time to take the kids to the parade downtown. I know Christmas didn't come that year. Or it could have been the year we stopped going to the Christmas Eve service and decided to watch the Christmas story on TV. The one on TV is so much prettier.

We have a beautiful manger scene on the coffee table. It has lots of animals, the wise men, and the shepherds, and Mary and Joseph. I bumped the table yesterday and the Baby fell out of the manger and shattered. You wouldn't even notice it if I hadn't told you.

I hope Christmas will come this year - it's been so long.

The Search

At the end of a long, hot day, the sun is finally creeping below the horizon. At the leader's signal, the caravan comes to a halt, and the riders crawl down from their beasts. As they set up their tents and prepare the meal, they feel the temperature dropping rapidly. In a short time they will be covering themselves with blankets to shut out the cold wind.

Sitting around the fire, they eat slowly, resting their weary and dusty bodies. Each eye shows a gleam of a purpose that calls them to something much greater than themselves. Though they speak no words, the glances they exchange speak for them.

As the dusk turns to darkness, all eyes turn to the sky above. Patiently they wait and continue to study the heavens, and then a smile brightens each face. It's still there - the Star! A new strength flows into their limbs as they gaze upon their blazing guide.

The days and months stretch on. They pause only to eat and to take a little rest. The search calls them forward; they cannot stop.

And finally they arrive at their destination. The search has come to an end, and the star never failed them. These men of wealth and royalty stand before a Child. With joy and with trembling, they lay their gifts before Him and worship the Son of God.

For months, possibly years, they labored unceasingly to follow the star. Years older, broken in body, they return to their homes penniless. They gave the very best they possessed. Their lives are now fulfilled; they return only to share the miraculous news that they actually beheld the Son of God and worshipped at His feet.

These few men gave their all, their strength, their labor, their fortunes without regret and without complaint. But what have we learned from their example? We won't give 15 minutes to read God's Word. We won't walk across the street to enter His house. Is it any wonder that our lives are empty and meaningless?

But they followed the star. The search consumed them. They would not, they could not turn back. Even today, wise men still seek Jesus.

The Light in Willie's Eyes

I walk down the hall passing several patients in wheelchairs, sharing a smile or a "Good morning" with those I know. "Hi, Miss Ellie. You want to come to the dayroom? We're going to sing some hymns in a few minutes." My steps create echoes down the silent hallway of shining white linoleum. Everywhere is the antiseptic smell of a hospital.

At the nurse's station, the staff all say hello and smile at me. They nod before I turn down another hallway. I need no other permission to drop into rooms or to wheel some patients to the dayroom. I knock on the door and speak before I enter one room, "Willie? How are you today?" Inside the dark room sits a little silver-haired man. He needs a shave and his shirt is buttoned up crooked.

"Barry!" he calls. He sits up a bit taller in his wheelchair and a smile broadens his face. "I was hoping you would come today." He asks me how I am as I straighten up his clothes just a bit before we leave the room. I help him put on his favorite sweater. His left arm hangs limp from a stroke several years ago.

"Where are your glasses, Willie?" He often takes them off inside his room. I don't think they are comfortable; they only serve to cover up his unseeing eyes for the sake of others.

Willie is one of several friends I visit most Saturdays. This little nursing home is only a 30-minute drive from college. I bring my guitar and we sing a few hymns together. Everyone has a favorite hymn and we sing a verse from all of them. They tell me about family and doctor visits and show me pictures of grandchildren. They seem as happy to see me as if I were a long lost child.

As I prepare to leave, Willie calls me to his side. "Barry, can you get me a Bible?"

This is going to be a challenge. "What grade of Braille do you read, Willie?" He told me to ask for grade 2.5, but I don't know if that means the size of the dots or the level of contractions used in Braille.

Each week Willie asked me about the Bible, and each time I saw his disappointment when I told him I was still looking. He had just about given up hope when a large package arrived one day addressed to Mr. Willie Randall.

The attendant carried the box down the long hall to Willie's room; "Willie, you've got a package. It's from the American Bible Society." The attendant placed the large box on his bed and opened it as Willie waited expectantly. "It's full of notebooks," he told Willie. A note inside explained that the 10 volumes contained the New Testament and Psalms.

Willie reached over and felt the spines of the large notebooks. He ran his finger over them and selected one at random. "Put this one on my lap," Willie asked.

Once the bulky binder was on his lap, Willie struggled to reposition his unresponsive left arm. He flipped the book open and began running his fingers over the raised dots, to decipher the words that only he could read.

`Willie's head was erect and his voice grew strong as he read aloud.

"*The people which sat in darkness have seen a great light; and to them which sat in the region and shadow of death light is sprung up.*"The attendant stood in awe as a tear trickled down his face. He quietly backed out of the room as Willie continued reading.

In a matter of minutes, the entire staff of the nursing home had heard about Willie's Bible and the verse it fell open to. A small group crowded into Willie's room to listen to him read. It seemed that one verse was a message to every caregiver, nurse, and patient alike. It said that God cares even about a tiny old man, a blind stroke victim who can't even dress himself without assistance. And if God cares for Willie, He must care for me, too.

I continued to visit that nursing home almost every Saturday while I attended college. Willie's smile was a little bit bigger, and his face seemed to shine, but maybe it was just my imagination. In a few years most of the people I had known and been close to passed away. But I will never forget the light in Willie's eyes.

A Clearer View

In our lives certain events become milestones. As time passes a battle to understand or to overcome an obstacle gains more and more significance. Much later we will recall other events as preceding or following these milestones. I would like to tell you about one of my milestones.

During my teens, encountering a group of Christians my own age helped bring excitement into my faith. We enjoyed home Bible studies, Scripture songs, and retreats. Throughout college we remained a tight-knit fellowship, supporting and encouraging one another.

In this environment, like a tropical greenhouse, I flourished. I read my Bible, and I devoured hundreds of inspirational books. Praying and listening, I constantly hungered for more of God's Presence in my life.

After graduation I began work while still attending church and a home Bible study. But gradually it seemed something was missing; still performing my same daily meditations, I no longer felt the Presence. The same Bible which before always breathed life to me, now read like dusty pages. Redoubling my efforts, I still felt nothing.

What could be the cause for this wilderness? Was I hiding a sin or a secret grudge to grieve the Spirit? But I found no cause. Even after long prayers and repentance the heavens remained impenetrable; I could not break through to make my prayers be heard. I walked a barren dessert, longing for a cool drink of water.

After months in this condition, I yearned to regain my sense of direction and of His Presence. I believed God was still there, but my feelings were completely void and numb. I took a few days off work for a private retreat.

I arrived at a tiny cabin in Black Mountain, North Carolina, and settled in for several days of quiet searching. No television, no radio, no people, no distractions. "I'll not leave until I have heard from God," I announced to the empty room. I unpacked my Bible, a huge concordance, and biographies of famous men of faith, hoping one of them held the secret to take me back to my previous state.

Day after day, I read, paced back and forth, and prayed aloud. Despairing at the loss of His Presence, I begged to know what prevented me from hearing Him. Still I felt no release.

My time was rapidly slipping away; the last morning dawned and still I felt the same as the day I arrived. I read and prayed until lunchtime had come and gone. In a few hours I would have to load the car and drive away. My frustration increased as I feared returning with no change in my devotional life. How long would I walk in this wasteland? I despaired at the thought of weeks, months, or even years in this state.

Going for a walk seemed like a good idea. Perhaps some fresh air and exercise would clear my mind. I wandered up and down the narrow steep streets of Montreat with no particular direction. After an hour of aimless strolling, I found myself at the base of a dirt road leading to Lookout Mountain.

When I read the simple sign pointing to the trail. a sudden rush came over me, accompanied by a sense of expectancy. An irresistible urge was calling me. I HAD to climb that mountain.

A wide muddy road led to the foot of the mountain. Surveying the trail, I had no idea how long the climb would be. The trail beneath ran under a canopy of tall trees, blocking out the sky. All about me were footprints and litter as evidence of many who had been here. As I began hiking, I soon noticed a change; each time the trail became steeper, the signs of wear and the litter decreased.

As the road narrowed to a broad path, something drew me upward. Anticipation grew stronger with each step. Each time the path took a sudden upturn, there were signs that others had stopped, rested, and turned back. At each new obstacle, the path narrowed.

Now it was a mere foot path, one seldom traveled. The surrounding brush closed in, making the climb more difficult. A little further, it was no longer a walk; it became a hand-and-foot climb over stones and roots. The brush yielded vines to help pull myself upward.

At this point there was no evidence of other hikers, no footprints, no soda cans or candy wrappers. How long had it been since someone had been here? A few minutes, an hour, a day? The thought of going where few had preceded increased my determination. There was no turning back.

Abruptly the cover of the trees opened and I struggled upward into the sunlight. The last 50 yards to the summit were the most grueling. At this point there were not even any vines to grasp; I crawled hand and foot over jagged stones to the crest.

Finally, the end of the journey had arrived. I sat on the highest point for miles around. Examining the view, I paused and caught my breath, slowly scanning from side to side. Everything below looked different from this point of view.

As I viewed the panorama, a realization dawned on me. From this perspective I saw beyond myself and my trivial concerns. Was it the still small voice I heard or was it my own imagination speaking?

I reconsidered my climb from the beginning to end. Isn't the way of the world wide, open, and easy? Isn't the way of the Lord narrow and difficult? Don't many become discouraged and turn back to the easier path? Doesn't walking with the Lord become difficult as you leave more of the world behind?

I thought of the similarities of the climb to my walk with the Lord. My faith had been easy in the hot house environment I had known. Am I willing to walk the narrow way? It will probably be lonely. Am I willing to make a path where others have not been? It will probably be difficult. Will I walk with the Lord, even if others reject me, even if I walk alone? Am I willing to walk in obedience, even if I never feel His presence again?

I stayed on the mountaintop for some time, considering those questions and reviewing my life. I concluded that I would rather live a difficult life with God's approval than an easy, undemanding life with the crowd.

When I descended the mountain and returned to the cabin, I had a sense of clarity. Perhaps I had only discarded some childish ideas, some need for excitement in my devotional life. But I came away with a sense of purpose that has never left me.

Over the years I have remembered that mountain retreat as a milestone in my faith, a time when I put aside some of my simpler ways and became more serious about walking the way of obedience.

Treading on Holy Ground

Some years ago, I was invited to attend a two day motivational seminar at Winthrop University in Rock Hill, South Carolina. I was feeling a bit discouraged with my work, and the workshop was just the shot in the arm I needed.

It was there I first met Regina Hannaghan. Regina was chatting with a tiny woman in a wheelchair who suffered from a rare condition in which the long bones of the body never fully developed. She then turned and finger spelled into the hand of a person both deaf and blind. Once she pivoted and her face came into view, I discovered that Regina was blind. A few decades ago doctors prescribed pure oxygen to infants born blue, not realizing that it often destroyed the optic nerve; this practice had forever removed sight from Regina's eyes.

But among this group I noticed an electricity. Their communication was rapid, excited, and charismatic. Each had a glow that set him or her apart from the crowd. Everyone attending the workshop wanted to chat with or at least meet one of these special people.

As the crowd thinned, I struck up a conversation with Regina. We decided to have lunch together, and she asked me to drive by her apartment so she could pick up a sweater.

A perky little terrier greeted us inside the door, and an orange tabby meowed his 'hello' as well. I stood in the tiny little kitchen as Regina prepared a bowl for the cat and for the dog. A green and yellow parakeet began to twitter, asking to be noticed as well. Regina spoke to the colorful little bird, which trilled at the sound of his name, and poured him a small amount of seed and water.

I helped Regina choose a sweater which would match her other clothing, and she asked me, "Would you like to hear my animals sing?"

I was a bit puzzled at her question, thinking she might be pulling my leg, but decided to play along. "Sure," I answered, "I'd love to hear them sing."

And then, something strange and wonderful happened. Regina began singing the words to a well known worship chorus. In seconds her gentle expression evolved from happiness to joy to worship. As she sang, the animals joined in. The dog leaned back and howled in time with the words, the cat meowed, and the bird bobbed up and down and sang its little heart out. They were literally joining in the song and participating in the worship.

A chill ran up my spine as the hair rose on the back of my neck and goosebumps appeared on my arms. I took a step back, trembling at the power I beheld, fearfully realizing that I stood on holy ground. I was witnessing a unity, a joining of all creation in praise to the Father as when the morning stars sang at creation.

I was dumbstruck at the beauty of the scene I was witnessing. Regina's face glowed, shining from a powerful light within bursting to get out. She was a living fulfillment of her name, a child of the King. Regina served a holy Master. I stood in awe at one of His handmaidens.

She finished the song, and after a short drive we enjoyed a pleasant lunch together. I remained friends with Regina for several years until we eventually lost track of one another. But I will always remember how this woman was in tune with the Almighty. Within this fragile vessel dwelt a great and wonderful power.

Inspiration Point:
Maintaining Connection with your Power Source

From time to time we all find ourselves in state of malaise, going through the motions of our lives and jobs with little sense of purpose or motivation. We get up and go to work to bring home the paycheck, to pay the bills, and go to bed to start all over again the following day. It is a pitiful existence when work and care of home and family becomes drudgery, when the light in our eyes dims and we work only to maintain the status quo.

I don't usually arrive in such a state overnight. It is a gradual and slow decline, a loss of excitement, a wearing down of energy, an ebbing of concern and care about myself and others. I wish I could always remain encouraged, excited, and optimistic, but I don't think it is human nature to do so. We tend to lose our sense of purpose and must wander about and find ourselves anew from time to time.

When I recognize that I have arrived at such a state, it takes a while to return to my Source of power and inspiration. I actually draw my strength from many small things, but I see them all as signs and manifestations of my Creator. He is my true Source of strength and hope. All my efforts are ways that I seek Him and try to communicate with Him.

I have always been drawn to the water. When I am troubled, nothing can bring me to a quiet and relaxed state like visiting a body of water. Beside a pond, a lake, or a stream I can sit, unwind, and untangle my troubles. In the city there are plenty of fountains, but they are seldom in places suitable for quiet meditation. A natural setting is the best location for me to ponder.

Beside a stream, a lake, a waterfall, I hear the gurgling or lapping sounds of the water. I look at the shimmering of the light striking the water and forget my everyday monotony. Rippling reflections of light and shadow speak to me of beauty; the beepers, buzzers and bells of work are far, far away. In the quiet I can focus, I can be still, and I can renew my connection with the Almighty.

I see His hand, I hear His voice in many circumstances, but I still seek out places of simple beauty to listen. Maybe it is a slow walk down a wooded path. It might be sitting beside a stream. In the mountains of North Carolina, I can overlook miles of forests, roads, bridges and streams stretched out to the horizon. I can select a high point and watch, letting all my worries dissolve. Against this panorama, my pitiful little anxieties fade away to insignificance.

Where do you reconnect with your power source? Is it walking down a garden path, studying the flight of bees and birds? Or is it more like my own retreat, resting and meditating by a body of water? Or is it sitting alone on a pew, thinking or reading, as you bask in the colored light falling upon you from a stained-glass window? Or maybe it is in your own backyard, sitting in an easy chair and enjoying a glass of iced tea as you watch the sun descend for his night's repose.

Whatever your method, whatever the place, we all need to find the time to reconnect with our Power Source, to make the journey to our personal Inspiration Point. We are not designed to work and live without meaning, automatons without feelings or purpose. If you find that you are just going through the motions, try to plan the time and place to get away, to reconnect, to refresh and renew your lifeline, to redefine your purpose.

My Own Private Gallery

We have often heard it said, "Beauty is in the eye of the beholder." People interpret this axiom with varied meanings. I find many traditional things beautiful; and then there are some which I just don't understand.

Personally, I don't see the beauty of many sports. Although I respect the work and sweat which go into a football game, running back and forth chasing a ball just doesn't strike me as beautiful. Watching cars race around and around the track seeing who passes whom and waiting for a crash doesn't do anything for me, either.

On the other hand, I see beautiful things every single day. On my drive to work I notice the first spring colors, the lush green of watered gardens, and the changing of the leaves during fall. On my monthly drive to visit my parents, I admire the rolling hills and the miles of green forests. I slow down at each river and creek I cross, looking for reflections on the flowing waters.

Is anything more mesmerizing than a thunderstorm? I love to watch the flashes of lightning race across a dark, threatening sky. For many years I have taken pleasure in sitting on a sheltered porch, watching the rain, feeling the cool breeze, and enjoying the smells and sounds of a hard rain accompanied by lightning and thunder.

At least for a few minutes each day I behold beauty in some form. I look through many windows at work, and I frequently glance to the sky. I am drawn to rolling clouds and especially to sunsets. Every night there is a show, a brilliant display of rapidly changing light and color. Almost daily I point out a colorful sky to a customer and watch him pause a few moments, stunned at the glory of a sunset he had blindly ignored.

There is another kind of beauty I see as well. I admire attractive people, and I see many different complexions and physiques daily. But there is something else about people which I find beautiful. Everyone seems to notice the beauty of an infant, and men tend to ogle attractive young ladies, but this superficial view of beauty is not what I mean. When I observe a couple, two people who are longtime companions, I am captivated by their interactions. The way each looks to the other's needs, they way he helps her stand, or the way she pauses and waits for him. Maybe one walks with a cane, and the other leans to support him; this is another unnoticed beauty.

Beauty IS in the eye of the beholder. Open your eyes and look more closely. Take a minute to observe and find something you didn't notice before. Try to find an unseen splendor. Maybe you, too, will find your own private gallery.

The Right Tool for the Job

Years ago I learned an electric fan would drown out a variety of noises and help me sleep. That habit has stayed with me, and now a dark room and the sound of a fan will send me into slumber in just a few moments.

When my trusty fan began grinding its gears in the middle of the night, I jumped out of bed wondering what airplane had landed on my lawn. No amount of oil could silence the horrible noise, and I discovered I am so conditioned to the fan drowning out the sounds from the street that I was unable to sleep.

I arose to search for anything in the house which could create that soothing noise so I might sleep. I have plenty of noisy devices, but none of them was appropriate. I am not made drowsy by the sounds of television or radio. And the blender, microwave, and the mixer all produced sounds unsuitable for inducing slumber. In my storeroom I saw a drill, a skill saw, and a leaf blower, but of course, none of them was even worth trying.

I needed a fan and nothing else. I tossed and turned through the night, planning an early morning excursion to Walmart to purchase another fan.

The next night, the comforting whir of a new fan lulled me into a restful slumber in no time. How wonderful it is when you have the right tool for the job.

And now, when I see people struggling with their work, I wonder - are you the right tool for this job? You can't drive a nail with a screwdriver, and a vise-grip is of little use when you need a plunger.

You don't go to Jiffy Lube for a cold, and you don't call your doctor when your roof leaks.

And I look at myself in my own job. Am I the right tool for this task? Do I do my job well? Do I perform better as a leader or a follower? Can I work well as part of a team? Or do I accomplish more working alone? Am I happy in my job, and is my boss pleased? Or would I be happier and would my efforts be more productive in a completely different setting?

The same questions apply to my devotional life as well. Lord, am I trying to be a pair of pliers when you really made me a crowbar? Am I seeking the wrong person in my life to accomplish the wrong task? Lord, give me the vision, give me the understanding to be the right tool in the lives around me. Give me the wisdom to recognize when I see the right person. Help me stop trying to shape people into what they are not meant to be. Lord, let me take my right place in the toolbox and not compete with the other tools. Help me to recognize what I am and to be the right tool for the job.

The Song Indescribable

I have heard a song, a mysterious floating melody, and its beauty is beyond comparison. At first I didn't understand the notes, I didn't even comprehend that it WAS a song. It's difficult to follow and requires full attention to hear above noise and distractions.

Several years ago I first heard it, a few delicate sounds whistling in a summer breeze. They sounded like colorful wildflowers and sunlight captured in a few quick notes. A few days later I caught a little more as I sat watching the night sky. Over the still of darkness I heard the comfort of a mother rocking her child to sleep.

As I listened closely, I recognized more bits of the song. I discerned the deep plaintive notes of a dirge as the frost drained the life from the last flowers refusing to bow their heads to the cool of autumn. I heard the clash of cymbals and roll of tympani as a thunderstorm split the sky from end to end.

I listened to strange interwoven harmonies as the birds sang their soprano complaints overhead to the bass undertones of the leaves crunching underneath my feet.

In the hush of a falling snow I could hear the rise and fall of laughter, like sleigh bells and Christmas carols. In the crackle of a dwindling fire, whispered gentle notes came to my ears, like the sighs of two people in love, resting in their embrace.

Over time many short measures of a long wandering melody came to me. As I paused beside a lush green meadow during a spring sunset, I heard the notes of deep rest and peace as a child whispered, "Now I lay me down to sleep." And notes of joy and excitement sang as two people looked deeply into one another's eyes and said, "I do."

The song continued into a slower movement; in the falling leaves I caught bittersweet sounds of sorrow and regret as someone wept, "I'm sorry. Please forgive me." And carried on the flutter of a butterfly's wings there were notes of hope as another softly answered, "Come home."

At times the notes grew strong and powerful like a military march. At others they slowed and deepened, resonating like a Gregorian chant. I was moved to tears as I heard the airy whisper of a deathbed confession, but my tears stopped as I perceived a message of hope carried in a resonant tune delivered on church bells.

Has the music grown more beautiful, or do I simply hear more clearly now? The musical score is now full. Notes delicate and light have combined with the deep rumbling bass, weaving themselves into a symphony - a hypnotic piece containing the joy of childhood, the mistakes and regrets of life, the fulfillment of a job well done, and the hope of more beyond the grave. I think I shall name it The Symphony of Life.

Spring Fever

It's been especially dismal this winter; day after day of frosty mornings and cold gray skies have taken a toll on my outlook. Even when the sky is clear, it's still cold. I'm tired of being cooped up inside warmed by dry heated air.

In my backyard is a large pile of leaves. As they fell day after day, I couldn't rake them fast enough. Then a week of cold rain brought more down. I gave up the losing battle, waiting for warmer weather to complete the task.

But finally I sense a change coming. The days are getting just a bit longer. The sunshine is a tiny bit warmer and the sky a little less gray. I observe the trees as I drive to work, anticipating buds and the first green leaf.

Soon, some warmer weather will be here, and I will expect to suffer a full blown case of spring fever. As soon as I see the daffodils in Mabel's yard I won't be able to resist.

First, I'll rake up all the leaves from the fall and winter. Then I will start picking out gardening supplies at the Home Depot. I will come home with fertilizer and mulch, seeds and seedlings.

I will get out and dig and plant and do too much. I will have aching muscles and a stiff back for several days, but I will still get out and walk about my yard every day, planning what I will do next.

I enjoy the beauty of the entire year, but I suppose spring fever is my attempt to participate in that beauty. I can dig and plant and cultivate, but it is still God who creates the beauty by causing everything to grow.

Too often, our souls are like the ground in winter. Inside, we have grown cold and everything is withered and lifeless. We need a spiritual spring fever, an excitement and urgent desire to grow and see beauty in our outward lives.

I suppose if I put the same cultivating effort into my life and relationships as I put into planting shrubs in my yard, my life would bear more fruit. People would notice something different in my demeanor, perhaps love, joy, peace, longsuffering, faith and meekness.

So this year, as I dig and cultivate my yard, bringing it out of a winter hibernation, I will devote a little more time to bringing my spirit out of hibernation as well.

The Hero in the Common Man

American culture is full of heroes. As children we learn about famous Americans and their contributions to our history. The virtues of George Washington and Abraham Lincoln as historic characters are extolled to kindergartners and elementary students.

A little later we learn of more contemporary figures whose lives typify sacrifice and standing up for personal beliefs. Martin Luther King, Jr. and John F. Kennedy stand as martyrs, people who died so that their ideals might be realized.

And should we run short of believable true personages, then we are given fictional heroes, even superheroes. An entire genre and subculture of literature surrounds the mythical exploits of humans with superhuman powers and even of mutants possessing supernatural abilities.

The natural conclusion of this pre-occupation with superhuman heroes is the dissatisfaction with normal everyday people. The person who simply lives a day to day life of family, work, and church is seen as insignificant, lacking any attributes worth admiration.

But I want to turn the tide, to change that point of view. I want to examine the common man to see if there is something of a hero in John Doe who lives on Maple Street.

John is not handsome, and he is not rich. He has a wife he married 33 years ago. Every day he still tells Mary she is beautiful. They have a daughter who left home and married. Their son who is going to tech school still lives at home; he works part-time in the evenings.

John works five days a week at an ordinary mill job. He brings home a paycheck that doesn't go as far as it used to. Mary works as a cashier at the grocery store, but it seems they give more hours to the younger and prettier cashiers.

John comes home from work everyday and rubs Mary's shoulders a few minutes before he sits and reads the mail. He may cut the grass or weed the garden a while before supper. Mabel, their neighbor, became a widow a few months ago. John cuts her grass every week without being asked.

John goes to church most Sundays. He puts a little money in the plate and listens to the preacher and bows his head and prays. If you asked him if he was a religious person, he would say no. He tries to read his Bible occasionally, but he doesn't understand much of what he reads. And he wouldn't say that he prays, but every day he looks up at the sky. He wishes for good things for the people around him. Occasionally he wishes a few good things for himself, but usually he just shakes those ideas off. He isn't that important; he will get by somehow.

Last year an acquaintance at work had cancer surgery and was out of work for some time. He used up all his sick leave and was too proud to accept charity. John and several buddies collected over $500 from all the workers. They dropped by together to cheer their friend up and just quietly left the money on the kitchen table when no one was watching.

John doesn't want much. He wants to pay his bills, to love his wife, to watch a little bit of television here and there. Occasionally he enjoys a cold beer after a hot day's work. He thinks Mary makes the most delicious pot roast and banana pudding on earth. Rarely will you hear a word of complaint out of him.

John isn't special. He isn't famous, rich, or handsome. But he is honest. And he is faithful.

American has a lot of Johns and Marys. They don't think of themselves as special, but they are. It is the stability and the honesty of average everyday people that makes us a stable, decent country. In his own way, John is a hero.

Christmas Came a Little Early this Year

Sales had been pitiful all night. With the threat of sleet and freezing rain, very few people were venturing into the cold, even for a hot BBQ buffet. It was 11:15, and there had been no customers for over two hours. We were all waiting for midnight so we could close.

As I sat watching the door, I scanned the decorations about the restaurant, but they gave me no cheer. I pondered how difficult this year had been.

My son lost his job and came back home, bringing with him clutter, confusion, and a pile of bills. My father passed away in late September. Massive changes at work, and frustrations and disappointments with a web-based business venture had taken a toll as well.

I looked out the window as the rain fell on the black pavement, longing for the joy of Christmas. My sense of expectation was gone. The bright hope I usually carry with me had dimmed to a low glimmer.

A car approached and parked. I stood with several menus, prepared to greet some late diners. But at the door appeared a woman in a raincoat, carrying a note and a cell phone. Her voice was quivering as tears filled her eyes.

"Have you seen an elderly man with a cane, asking for breakfast? My father left the nursing home and no one can find him," she said trembling.

I invited her in, asking her to tell me more. She choked back her tears as she explained. Two hours earlier he had stormed out, leaving to get some breakfast. He was gone before anyone could stop him. She had contacted the authorities and driven here, his favorite restaurant, watching both sides of the road frantically during the hour drive.

I attempted to calm her and dialed 911, giving her the phone to describe the situation. I asked a waitress to bring her a glass of water as she spoke with the dispatcher. Once the call was complete, I suggested she sit down for a few minutes and gather her thoughts.

She described a man much like my own father, and I understood his condition as it was like the onset of my own mother's Alzheimer's syndrome.

Relieved to speak with someone genuinely concerned, she gave me her home and cell phone numbers. I assured her if he arrived, I would contact her and keep him from leaving. As she paused at the door, I clasped her hand and looked into her eyes, "Try to remain calm. I'm certain God is watching over him. I'll be praying for you." She thanked me and left to continue her search.

I watched the doorway and parking lot constantly until we closed. Moving my paperwork to the cashier stand, I continued the vigil until every task was finished and it was time to leave. Driving home, I scanned the sides of the road as I prayed the gentleman would return safely. Lying in bed, I looked up into the darkness, silently wishing for angels to watch over him.

The following morning I contacted the daughter, and she excitedly told me he was safe and sound. In the rain and darkness, her father had made a wrong turn, eaten at another restaurant and then returned at 1:30 AM. Relieved that he was unharmed, I asked if the home had taken any new precautions in caring for him. She laughed and told me that he wouldn't be driving any longer, then thanked me repeatedly for my kindness and concern.

Once I knew he was out of danger, a great sense of peace enveloped me. I didn't really DO anything, but I was glad to have assisted one troubled soul. Seeing another in real need put my own worries in better perspective.

So Christmas came a little early for me. I don't need any fruitcake, and it won't bother me if I have no presents under the tree. My Christmas gift arrived when I was able to give a bit of hope to another in greater need than myself.

Chip and Ginny

It was 1976, and I was working in my first job after college as a 3rd Shift Supervisor at an institution for the intellectually disabled. My shift began at 11 pm and ended at 7 am. Having never worked 3rd shift for an extended period before, I found it exhausting to adjust to a different sleeping pattern. Emotionally as well it was quite an awakening to learn the patients; as a compassionate person, it was an assault on my senses to interact with so many children with severe handicaps and misshapen limbs. As supervisor I was responsible for the staffing and supervision of several units, altogether housing almost 300 clients.

Most of my staff were average people without much education; many of them struggled to make ends meet. As part of my responsibilities I made random bed checks to make sure the staff were actually doing their jobs - tending clients who were wet or soiled, bathe them, remake the beds, and put the clients back down to sleep. At times I found the job very troubling; walking by some beds the handicaps were obvious. Some slept in strange, unnatural positions or made noises even as they slept. A few rested without sleeping at all, just sitting quietly and rocking all night. As I walked past their beds with a flashlight, I often prayed silently for those who seemed the most afflicted.

One night late in the year I entered a ward and found one of my staff crying. She was in her 50's, a grandmother whose husband was disabled after a severe heart attack.

"Ginny, what's wrong?" I asked. She revealed worries about Chip, her grandson. I knew the 2-year old had been ill for some time and was in the hospital for tests.

Ginny wiped her eyes, turning away as she answered. "Chip has leukemia. It's a rare strain, and it usually only affects adults." I learned they were starting chemotherapy in hope of throwing the illness into remission.

"Ginny, you are too upset to work. I will get someone else to cover this ward. Wrap up your paperwork and get ready to go home," were my directions to her. "I'll be praying for Chip," I told Ginny as she left.

Many nights I found Ginny crying. Chip was taken to the Duke University Hospital. He did not respond to the first round of chemotherapy, and after a week's rest another 30-day round was begun. Now all the possible side effects appeared. Chip was weak with vomiting and nausea. His hair fell out. I asked Ginny for a photo of Chip before he became ill and took it to the Bible study I attended every week.

Day after day I prayed for Chip; I had never met him, but I felt strongly attached to him. The 2nd round of chemotherapy was complete, and there was no improvement, no sign of remission. The doctors said another series would be of no use.

December was already here, and Christmas was fast approaching. Chip's parents hardly slept between working and staying with their child. The nurses were doing their best to bolster Chip's strength so he could go home for Christmas day.

"What do you want for Christmas?" his parents asked. After thinking briefly, Chip answered. "I want a pony." Ginny knew the parents were already struggling financially; she intended to buy him a rocking horse or a toy pony. Somehow his dad scraped up the money and bought a live Shetland, keeping it a secret for that special morning.

But on Christmas eve, Chip took a negative turn. He was too weak to go home even for part of Christmas Day. Ginny and I both wept. I don't know how his parents could bear this.

Chip was just hanging on, getting weaker by the day. I brought his name up at the Bible study for prayer over and over again. No one else seemed to have the concern I did.

Soon Ginny told me the doctors reported there was nothing else they could do. Chip didn't have much time left. Every instance when Ginny had two days off she went to NC to be with her son and with Chip. The following morning after work her husband would drive her to Duke while she slept.

It was almost daylight when I completed work and went to my little apartment, but I could not go to bed. I remember getting on my knees and arguing with God as the morning light streamed in my bedroom window. I had the strong impression that God had a special purpose for Chip and that the devil was trying to destroy him.

The only word to describe what I experienced is wrestling; I felt I was in a tooth and nail struggle - and I refused to let go. I don't know how long I prayed, but suddenly I felt something snap. I had a tremendous release and felt the battle had been won. I finally lay down and slept with a smile on my face.

I was on pins and needles until Ginny returned to work 3 nights later. There were no cell phones in that day, and I had no way to contact her. Finally Ginny returned to work running down the hallway.

"Something has happened I know!" I exclaimed. "Tell me - tell me!"

Ginny was out of breath and so excited. "The doctors can't explain it. They said it was like the disease had been cut in half. He's suddenly better."

Each day Chip improved and was soon able to go home. The doctors told the parents, "He is a miracle baby. Nothing we did helped him. God healed this child." His case was even described in detail in a medical journal. Chip was taken back for several checkups, but there was never any sign of the leukemia returning.

Recently after more than 30 years I have been in touch with Ginny AND with Chip. I talked with him on the phone at length and learned a few details that were previously unknown to me.

When Chip was released from the hospital, he was still weak. Ginny told me that one evening she sat in a rocking chair looking through a Bible story book with Chip. She was puzzled because even though this was a new book he had never seen before, Chip was able to identify various Bible characters and already knew their stories. Ginny was weeping as they looked at the pictures. Chip looked up at her and said, 'Don't worry, Gramma. I'm not going to die. Jesus took me to heaven and talked with me. He told me I had to come back."

During chemotherapy the doctors warned the parents that if Chip survived that he would never be able to father children; the harsh treatments would make him sterile. Chip is now married, lives in Tennessee, and is a successful home builder. By the way, he has two beautiful sons ages 5 and 8. We haven't made specific plans yet, but in the near future I hope to meet Chip and spend some time with him, his precious wife and children.

CHAPTER 3

Mom and Dad

Magical Train Ride

T he imagination and the exuberance of childhood are thrilling to behold, and if you can regain even a tiny portion of your childhood
excitement, it is wonderful to possess.

In Boone North Carolina, is an attraction - maybe you would say it's
just a tourist trap - but it holds a special place in my memory. Tweetsie
Railroad is a small amusement park, centered around an old steam locomotive. The events are more politically correct now, but when it opened
in the 1950's, the train was regularly attacked by robbers and Indians.

I was just a small child, five-years-old, familiar with the Lone Ranger
and the Cisco Kid, when my parents took me to Tweetsie. We saw a black-
smith shop, an old print shop, a saloon and some dancehall girls.

We took a stroll through the general store looking for souvenirs before the next scheduled train ride. It was there I discovered an amazing thing, a double-barreled popgun, complete with two triggers, two corks and two strings. This was quite an exciting find, something to show everyone at kindergarten. Mama and Daddy bought me the toy, and I pulled the triggers and popped the corks over and over while we anticipated the next departure.

We didn't have long to wait. The conductor descended the steps and yelled "All aboard" in typical fashion. We took our places on the wooden seats; I sat excitedly by the window. We could smell the smoke from the engine and hear the puffs of steam as the locomotive built up pressure. In a few minutes we heard the chug-chug-chug, just like in the movies, and after the first quick jerk, the train slowly pulled out of the station.

There were some interesting sights during the ride. Leaning out the window yielded a frightening view when the train crossed a wooden trestle. The conductor pointed out moonshiners and their still, and we heard gunshots as they chased off "revenuers." We were warned that bandits might try to rob the train and about a tribe of Indians who were on the warpath. They had scalped several settlers just a few days ago. I sat nervously on the seat, holding my popgun tightly.

Just as we were warned, bandits in masks chased the train on their horses. I watched open-mouthed as they removed a money box from the mail car and shot the lock off. But just in time, the sheriff arrived with his posse and captured the gang.

With the money box safe onboard again, we continued our journey. In a few minutes I heard a blood-curdling sound. War whoops rang out from a band of Indians pursuing the train. They shot a flurry of arrows at the train, and the conductor and engineer fired back with their six-irons.

But the danger drew closer. The train stopped and more Indians arrived. They were running up to board the train. A gigantic redskin in headdress and loincloth, complete with warpaint and a tomahawk, entered our car with a loud whoop and was coming straight towards us. I pointed my popgun at the savage and fired both barrels at once.

Immediately the Indian clutched his chest and fell to the floor. He didn't move again. Stunned, I looked at the popgun in my hands.

In moments the battle was over. The sheriff and some cowboys arrived, shooting a few Indians while the remainder escaped on horseback. The conductor dragged the dead Indian out of our car. I sat quiet and still during the ride back to the station.

When we stepped down to the platform, Daddy asked me how I liked the ride. I don't remember all the details, but I do remember telling him to take the gun back to the store, that it was too dangerous for me.

The trip to Tweetsie has held a magic for me and my family ever since, almost 50 years now. Tweetsie Railroad still runs and carries passengers around the track, and the general store and the saloon are still there.

My son Nathan and I visited Tweetsie when he was five years old. I smiled and chuckled as he rode the train with excitement. And I now have a grandson, the twinkle of my eye. I hope to take him to Tweetsie, so I can watch the excitement and live it again through his eyes. I hope his ride on Tweetsie will be as magical as mine was.

The Old Man and the Lake

It's 1964. I am sitting in Miss Agnes Davis's 4th grade classroom, ready to bolt out the door as soon as the 2:30 bell rings. It's Tuesday; Daddy will get off work early and take me and my brother fishing.

Finally the bell sounds and I race out the door and down the stairs of Hampton Street School. Across the vacant lot, across the street and the railroad tracks, I run to our little house with hardly a break in speed.

First, I have homework to do (Daddy won't take us if it isn't done), and then I have to clean up my room. Maybe I can dig for worms before

Daddy gets home. Brent gets home from junior high school and quietly begins his homework. He did his chores this morning.

I finish the homework and make a whirlwind sweep at my chores before flying out the backdoor holding a coffee can and a spoon. I go straight to Mama's hydrangea bushes and start digging for worms.

Daddy soon arrives home and I run to meet him. He scoops me into his arms and rubs his stubbly face all over my neck. I giggle and squirm as he says with a laugh, "I'm going to whiskerize you!"

After he confirms that homework and chores are done, Daddy gathers his tackle box, rod and reel, and two bamboo poles. He drives just a few blocks and stops at the ice house. Daddy places the big cooler on the platform, signaling the man to drop a block of ice into the chopper. Soon our bottles of soda are covered with shimmering chips.

Finally we are traveling down a narrow two-lane road, passing through communities too small to have a caution light. Approaching Lake Greenwood, we turn onto a smaller road and search for a dirt and gravel driveway almost swallowed up by the undergrowth.

The brush clears to reveal a small shack and a little yard bordering the lake. I see a tiny chicken coop, a small garden, an old limping dog who always barks when we drive up, and Mr. Patterson. He stops digging in his little garden, dropping the hoe and hurrying toward the car.

He wears an old pair of patched khakis, a t-shirt, wading boots, and a pith helmet. His wrinkled face is tanned and tough like leather; he always wears several days growth of gray whiskers.

Mr. Patterson calls Brent and me by name and opens the car door. We grab the can of worms and poles and head for the lake; Dad and Mr. Patterson get the cooler and follow more slowly.

While Brent and I fumble with the corks and worms and bamboo poles, Daddy casts his line to test a new lure. He and Mr. Patterson talk quietly as they watch their lines; Brent and I frequently jerk our lines from the water and switch positions, each convinced the other has the spot where the bigger fish are biting.

Soon the sun begins to descend, and the men meander toward the little one-room shack. Brent and I continue fishing until we can no longer see our corks in the water.

We enter the little hut lit by a single bulb hanging from the rafters. The little shack is warm inside, but it always smells of kerosene. The outer walls are made of tarpaper and shingles; inside the walls are coated with newspaper to keep out the drafts. There's an old squeaky bed, a small dresser, a fridge Mr. Patterson calls a Kelvinator, a hot plate, a few shelves. He has no inside plumbing. He washes his dishes in a pan he fills from a spigot outside. There is no bathroom, just a little outhouse.

Daddy and Mr. Patterson are deep in discussion completely beyond the comprehension of two young boys. Mr. Patterson moves the huge tattered Bible from his lap to the bed. He leaves a marker on the page so they can return to their conversation later.

Mr. Patterson offers a prayer of thanks for the food and then presents a plate full of fried fish and a few fried potatoes. Out of our catch, Mr. Patterson has created a small feast. We sit on rickety cane-bottom chairs as we happily eat from paper towels.

Afterwards, Brent and I return outside to chase lightning bugs and play hide-and-seek until time to leave. When we crawl into the car, Daddy leaves most of our catch with Mr. Patterson, keeping just enough to make one more meal at home with Mama. As they shake hands, Daddy slips him some money to help buy groceries.

Mr. Patterson reaches into the car to pat us two boys on the head and says a little prayer for our safe travel home. I will be sleeping before we reach the highway.

We made that 30-mile drive to visit Mr. Patterson weekly for nearly two years. He lived alone, unsupported by his family, on a small government stipend. I recall him affectionately, an older man, struggling to keep himself alive, happy to share with two young boys, and thankful for the simplest kindness shown him.

I remember those weekly visits fondly, and I am thankful for the wisdom of my father to let his two sons share in the life of this old man. Perhaps it was those visits which instilled in me a love for the water, for the beauty of nature, and my respect for the older generation. Much of my life today was shaped by the time I spent with the Old Man and the Lake.

Daddy Versus GE

There are many things I could say about my father; I could describe to you his gentleness, his honesty, or his planning for the future. I could tell you of his love for the church and his years of dedication. I know stories of his patience, his persistence, and his years of labor in customer service operating a drycleaners and laundry in a small town.

I cannot remember a single instance of Daddy losing his temper. Only once did I ever hear a profane word come out of his mouth. And even then, he wasn't actually cussing; he was making a point to me as a teenager and asking me which sounded more intelligent. "How would you be thought of if you said, 'The pain was excruciating' compared to 'It hurt like #%#$*.'" 40 years later I still rarely use profanity.

Only once did I ever see any form of alcohol in our home. I was nine years old and sick with the croup. After two sleepless nights of hearing constant coughing, Daddy brought home a small bottle of whiskey. He gave me a few drops on a spoonful of sugar. The coughing stopped, and everyone slept peacefully that night.

But rather than be too serious, I would like to tell you about the time Daddy tackled General Electric Corporation - and WON!

In August of 1975 Mama's built-in oven was on the fritz. When H.D. Payne Company sent a repairman to our home, he found the problem quickly. Replacing a worn-out thermostat was all that was necessary. The repairman returned to the office to pick up the thermostat, but he soon returned, explaining that the part was out of stock. He had placed it on order, and it should arrive in a few days.

When the serviceman had not returned in a few days, Daddy called to be certain our repair was not forgotten. He was told that the part was out of stock at the supply warehouse and was on backorder. The warehouse was expecting the shipment to arrive any day.

Daddy put it on his calendar, and every Monday he called back. "No, the thermostat is still on back-order. It hasn't come in yet." Daddy was always polite and diplomatic, but H. D. Payne Company soon tired of his weekly calls.

The problem continued through August, September, and October. Daddy called other service companies in Greenville, Spartanburg, and Columbia, hoping a larger repair service would have one of the missing thermostats in stock. He received the same unhappy news at every location.

November came, and Mama asked the neighbors if she could use their oven to cook our Thanksgiving turkey. Of course the neighbors were helpful, but it was a challenge cooking the turkey at one house, dressing and sweet potatoes at another, and working around their own separate holiday schedules. Daddy saw all the problems Mama was having and was resolved to put this situation to an end.

He made one more call the Monday after Thanksgiving, and I saw the disappointment on his face as he put the phone down. He sat at the desk, staring at the ceiling, his hands in a prayerful position tapping slowly at his chin; the chair squeaked as he slowly rocked back and forth. I could almost see the wheels turning as he sought the missing piece to this puzzle.

He suddenly sat upright and snapped his fingers. Picking up the phone, he began a series of phone calls, going up the chain-of-command until he had the name and address of the PRESIDENT of General Electric Corporation.

Daddy spun his chair around to face the old upright Royal typewriter. Daddy was a self-taught typist; although he only used two fingers, he could produce a letter in a matter of minutes. I heard the familiar tap tap tap on the paper and the loud ding signaling time to throw the carriage.

He soon finished his letter. He rolled out the page and examined each line carefully. It must have absolutely no errors.

Mr. Reginald H. Jones, President
General Electric Corporation

Dear Mr. Jones,

For many years as a homeowner I have bought and used General Electric appliances. In my home I have a GE refrigerator, range, oven, toaster, iron, and more. As a business owner I have a variety of General Electric appliances in use there as well.

For many years I have been very pleased with the quality and durability of these products and with the service I have received from General Electric, that is until recently.

In August my wife's built-in General Electric oven (model #ABC123) stopped working when the thermostat failed. I was told by the local repair company that the thermostat (item #XYZ789) was out of stock and on back-order.

Every week since then I have faithfully called H.D. Payne Company and been told every time that the thermostat has not arrived and is still on back-order. August, September, and October have passed. November arrived and we had no oven to cook a turkey for our Thanksgiving Dinner.

And now, Christmas is rapidly approaching and I fear we will not be able to cook a turkey for this family gathering as well.

Mr. Johnson, I feel certain that as big and prosperous as General Electric Corporation is there must be a box of these thermostats sitting on a shelf in some forgotten storeroom. It would be a shame if my family could not have their traditional Christmas dinner because of a misplaced thermostat.

I feel certain that with your encouragement, the GE parts department will be able to find the thermostat our serviceman needs and that *we will be able to enjoy our traditional Christmas dinner. I feel confident that you will prove that my long term faith in General Electric has not been in error.*

Thank you for your attention in this matter.

Sincerely,

Gary H. Holcomb

Daddy walked across the street to the post office and mailed the letter special delivery. He returned wearing a little smirk on his face. He looked at me with a smile as he rubbed his huge hands together. "Now, let's see what happens."

Just a few days later, Mama got a phone call. H.D. Payne had received the thermostat and would like to come and complete the repair job. In short time the thermostat was installed, and Mama was humming as she tested the oven by baking a pan of her delicious cornbread.

That afternoon, the doorbell rang. There was a service truck in the driveway from Columbia; the man at the door stated he was there to repair the oven. Mama explained it had been repaired that morning and thanked him anyway.

The next morning another service truck was in the driveway and the doorbell rang again. Mama turned away the serviceman from Spartanburg who had been sent to fix the oven. That afternoon a truck from Greenville arrived and was turned away. Over the next few days the phone rang frequently; Mama explained to a variety of people from several states that our oven had been repaired and that we no longer needed the thermostat. Three or four thermostats arrived by mail as well.

Daddy had solved the problem gloriously. That Christmas we laughed repeatedly as everyone went by the oven and peeked at the baking turkey and dressing. The oven and the thermostat were the topic of discussion Thanksgiving and Christmas for many years to come.

To this day I admire Daddy's ability to manage a business and a home with a minimum of stress and never a hateful or profane word spoken. I wish I had a fraction of the foresight and financial sense he had.

P.S. Daddy wrote a very nice thank you letter to Mr. Jones.

Make a Memory

Shuffling through some old photos, I paused when I spotted an object I hadn't seen in years. The Coca-Cola ice chest, made of insulated aluminum, brightly painted and heavy as a truck, was an essential part of numerous vacations and trips. Inside, a tray held sandwiches safely above the ice and drinks below. On the side was a bottle opener, with the same Coca-cola logo imprinted in the metal. The ice chest came from the era before sodas came in pop-top cans. Near the bottom a screw-off cap allowed us to collect a brisk drink of water from the slowly melting ice.

My parents were more frugal than most people are today; they were Depression Era children and always saved their pennies. They preferred to carry a meal on the road rather than to buy a prepared one.

Life ran at a different pace then. There were no fast food restaurants on every corner. There were no ATM's. Most gas stations closed at 6:00 pm Saturday and didn't open on Sunday. To make a weekend trip, you visited the bank on Friday. It was next to impossible to cash an out-of-town check.

But on trips, Mama always packed the ice chest with her special sandwiches, potato salad, deviled eggs, and fried chicken. We usually carried bottled drinks, but the treat was a special punch Mama made for picnics.

If we went to the mountains or the beach, we could count on a heavenly picnic on the way. It seemed there were roadside picnic tables around every bend. Inviting little rest stops, complete with a table and a grill, patiently waited for families to stop and enjoy a meal.

I guess picnics fell by the wayside because of the planning they require. You need to make sandwiches and a side dish. You have to buy ice and sodas. If you are making a trip, you probably don't want any additional tasks. No one wants to take the time for any of those things now. "Oh, we can eat at McDonald's on the way." And your meal will be as forgettable as every other fast food meal you've ever eaten.

I own a traditional style picnic basket which I used when the kids were small, on vacations and afternoon trips to the park. Maybe there is a playground or a zoo you could visit. Maybe there is a scenic route worth the drive. This fall I plan to visit the Blue Ridge Parkway when the leaves are showing their best color. Maybe it could just be a Sunday afternoon cookout. Having children is not a requirement for any of these activities.

When I showed my brother the photo, he had the same reaction I did. "I wonder what happened to that ice chest," he said. He recalled how we often opened it and peeked inside and rambled on about the meals Mama used to pack in that cooler.

Maybe this summer you can make a memory or to start a new family tradition. With a little planning, you could create a memory your family will treasure like I do mine.

The Honey-Do List

It seemed Mama always wanted some little thing around the house fixed, or moved, or rearranged. Daddy worked long hours and often answered, "I'll get to it soon."

Although I never saw Mama and Daddy argue, I guess one time she must have nagged him a bit about one of those fix-it jobs. In a stern voice I heard him say, "Just make a list. Write down every single thing you want done, big or small. Give me a list." He turned away and walked down the hallway to his office.

Excitedly Mama immediately began working on the list. She sat at the kitchen table with a pad and pencil and started writing down all the errands, repairs, and fix-its. From a leaky faucet to a new window shade, from weeding a flower bed, to silencing the squeak in the hallway floor, she wrote them all down.

The writing began furiously and continued for days, and I saw the list growing. As Mama was cooking or folding laundry, another item would come to mind. She would stop to hurriedly add one more thing to the list. What started as a few lines was now pages long.

After a few days, Daddy asked, "Is the list ready?" Mama answered that she needed more time to finish it.

Perhaps a month had passed when mysteriously the writing stopped. Mama didn't write any more, but the list was nowhere to be seen. And she failed to say anything to Daddy about starting on the work.

Daddy came home one day and asked Mama, "Show me your list. I can start working on it tomorrow." Mama suddenly blushed, mumbled something, and turned away.

Daddy thought this really strange and followed her. "What did you tell me?" he asked as he followed her from the kitchen, to the den, to the back porch.

Again she mumbled something as she turned away, making her comment impossible to understand. Finally, Daddy placed his hands on her shoulders and slowly turned her to face him as he asked, "Where is the list?"

Mama looked at him, and then looked downward. "I threw it away," she said softly. When he asked her why, she explained. "I wrote down everything, and when I saw how long it was, I was ashamed of myself. I threw it away."

Daddy hugged her tightly; they kissed, and then laughed. I didn't hear everything they said, but I later noticed Daddy tried a little harder to keep up on the chores, and Mama tried harder to make sure something was really needed before she asked Daddy for help.

I Thought of You Today, Mama

I thought about you today, Mama. For several days I've been thinking of my last visit. I hate it that I live two hours away, and I can only come once a month to see you. I am so glad Brent lives close by and visits you everyday.

But I was in the mall. I went to buy a birthday present for a friend and was on my way out. I was calmly riding the escalator when I saw it out of the corner of my eye.

I turned and stared, my jaw dropped, and suddenly I had to return to the floor above. I turned and scrambled up the descending stairs, past the complaining people - I didn't care what they said. I had to get back up the steps and buy it.

I stood in front of the display case and stared at it; it wasn't that pretty, just a green pitcher. But it was EXACTLY like the one you had.

I carefully reached in and picked it up. I held it delicately as though it were the rarest of crystal. Lifting it to eye level, I stared at the simple piece of pottery. And suddenly I was in another time and place.

It was 50 years ago; Brent and I were sitting at the picnic table in the backyard under the pecan tree. We waited excitedly and out you came, carrying a tray bearing a snack for a summer afternoon. A bowl of popcorn and a green pitcher filled with Kool-Aid made us royalty for the afternoon.

And I remember another time when I was sick with the flu; you brought me lunch in bed. There on the tray was soup and a sandwich, and on the table you left a glass and that pitcher filled with Kool-Aid.

I carried the pitcher to the cashier to make my purchase. It wasn't expensive, but the price didn't matter to me. I HAD to have it. I made sure the cashier packed it very carefully.

I stopped at the grocery store on the way home. One essential ingredient was missing.

At home I sat down in the living room, with the pitcher and a glass on a tray. I poured myself some cherry Kool-Aid and remembered you, and Brent, and the magical time of childhood and a mother's love.

I'll be down next week to visit you at the nursing home. Maybe you will recognize me this time. But even if you don't, I have a little surprise for you. I am bringing the pitcher with me. And you and I are going to share a glass of Kool-Aid.

A Handful of Flowers

I glance from the road to my wristwatch for the 50th time since leaving Charlotte. I push the speed limit, anxious to arrive in Columbia before 10 a.m. I fought through the rush hour traffic of Charlotte and managed to reach the interstate by 8:30.

I should arrive right on time, but I'm still anxious. It's been more than two months since I visited Mama; I feel guilty for being away so long. I fear she won't know me.

Work presses in on my mind. Yesterday I managed the restaurant from 8 am to 11 pm, and I didn't get in bed till after 1. Why are my night sales dropping? I really should remove two employees, but I don't have anyone to fill their places. I need to hire three more at least. And what problems will I face tomorrow?

I force work out of my mind and think about Mama. She hardly speaks at all now. And even though the bones have knit well, she has not walked since breaking her hip. Even with an aide supporting her on each side, she will not stand, fearing another fall.

I think of Mama in earlier days: how she sang in the choir, all the flower arrangements she made at Shealy's Florist - thousands upon thousands. She made wreaths for funerals, potted arrangements for hospital patients, bouquets and sprays for weddings, corsages and boutonnières for proms. There was no end.

She loved to cook - church suppers, cakes for birthdays, cookies for holidays - and occasionally she had the minister over for Sunday dinner. Constantly in and out of the kitchen, she circled the table filling everyone's glass and bringing hot rolls from the oven. And how she beamed when she brought out that special dessert.

Just a few more miles and I'll be there, and suddenly it dawns on me. I didn't get her a flower. I always stop and buy her a small potted plant; I don't care if it dies in a week as long as she gets some enjoyment out of it. But in my haste to leave, I forgot.

I'm already at the exit. I guess I'll find a grocery store and buy a small plant. But as I drive up the ramp, I see a flash of color in the grassy bank on the left. Wildflowers! Mama will like those. I pull off the side of the road and park. In a moment I am wading through the brambles to pick those colorful wildflowers.

It's a brilliant display of color - blue bachelor's buttons, yellow and white daisies, black-eyed susans, pink primroses, and something red that looks like a poppy. Here's a couple of white Queen Anne's lace. I collect a large handful and struggle back up the bank to the car. My only container is a paper cup, but it will have to do.

In a few minutes my brother and I are entering the nursing home. Walking down the hallway with my little bouquet of free flowers, we pass offices and meeting rooms. I cannot help but notice the elaborate arrangements and magnificent flowers decorating the home; gigantic chrysanthemums, delicate gloxinias, bright caladiums, lilies and massive ferns decorate every office and patient's room, looking down on my lowly wildflowers in a paper cup.

But there's no turning back now. We enter her room and see Mama has fallen asleep in her wheelchair. I touch her hand and speak to her. "Mama, I've come to see you."

She slowly raises her head and struggles to open her eyes. At first her eyes appear glassy and unknowing. I swallow the lump in my throat and speak again. Behind my back, I remove the flowers from the paper cup and hold them in my bare hand. "I brought you some flowers," I said, embarrassed at my pitiful gift.

But the bright colors have caught her eye. She reaches forward and takes the flowers from my hand. She lifts them into the light and close to her face. Her other hand rises and gnarled wrinkled fingers extend toward the simple blossoms. Gently and slowly she touches each and every flower, turning the bouquet and caressing each silky petal.

Her eyes twinkle, and a smile creases her weathered face. And her eyes turn toward me and she calls my name. Perhaps she remembers when I was a child, and many times I gave her a small handful of dandelions. Her smile grows as my eyes brim over.

Mama talked to me excitedly. I only understood a few words here and there, but she was happy to see me and delighted with the flowers. I held her hand tightly, and we chatted for a while. I talked about her cooking and the flower shop - and what she talked about I am not sure. But we connected and we communicated.

Soon she begins to tire. She has been out of bed several hours, and an aide will soon wheel her to the dining room. But she still holds her handful of flowers.

I called my brother a few days later. Mama has seemed brighter since my visit. And when he sees her each morning, at least once she says my name. I feared my visit would be too late and my gift too small, but I didn't take into account the power of a few kind words and a handful of flowers.

A Lifetime of Chocolate Bunnies

Holidays were always fun at our house. Every special day on the calendar meant something out of the ordinary, even if nothing more than a cake and a drive in the country.

But Easter was one of the biggest celebrations. It always meant new clothes for church, even down to new shoes. Easter Sunday all the ladies would be decorated like Easter eggs themselves, in colorful dresses, frilly lacy hats, and corsages. The men would wear new suits, some fidgeting at the starched collars, but still sporting new ties and boutonnières.

My brother and I hated the new clothes, but we tolerated them as part of the special day because we knew there would be baskets filled with goodies from the Easter Bunny. We loved the colorful dyed eggs, marshmallow chicks, candy eggs, maybe even a marzipan egg with a peephole revealing the scene inside. But most important without a doubt was the chocolate bunny.

But the year my brother turned 12, Mama concluded he was too old for an Easter basket. You cannot imagine the wailing we heard that Easter morning. Brent was crying and bellowing, absolutely inconsolable. Amidst all the tears and blubbering, the only intelligible words were, "chocolate bunny. I want my chocolate bunny."

Mama tried her best to console him so we could prepare for church, but there was no winning this battle. He HAD to have a chocolate bunny.

In 1962 no stores in town were open on Sunday. Gas stations, grocery stores, drugstores, everything was closed. Not until 1 pm would any business be open, and then only one small grocery store and one drugstore.

Attending church on Easter morning was an absolute necessity, and we could not go unless Brent got his chocolate bunny. Mama called the druggist Chick Pitts who lived around the corner, begging him to open Young's Pharmacy and sell her one chocolate Easter bunny. Having a child of his own he understood, and soon Mama was standing in front of Brent. In her hands she held the crucial confection.

His eyes were now dry and Brent looked expectantly, knowing he was about to receive his heart's desire. As she handed him the prized sweet she made a fateful promise. "As long as I live or am able, every Easter hereafter you WILL have a chocolate bunny."

During his teen years, getting a bunny each Easter embarrassed him. During his 20's, he didn't mind the little gift; he even looked forward to the joke of it.

A few years ago, as Mama's faculties declined, she no longer remembered Easter, colored eggs, or chocolate bunnies. But the love and affection she showed us, Brent has given back time and again, visiting daily at the nursing home and attending to her every need.

The circle is complete, and now Brent happily gives Mama a chocolate bunny at Easter.

The Changing of the Guard

I am sitting on the front pew of First Baptist Church of Clinton; I haven't been inside this church since my college days. It's Monday, September 22, 2003 - just a couple of days after my birthday. On my right is my brother Brent; on my left are my two kids, Adria and Nathan. We are gathered for Daddy's funeral. All of us are somber, but Nathan is the most uncomfortable; he has had a difficult time dealing with death ever since his mother passed away.

As we listen to the organ music, I ponder the last few years of Daddy's life. Gary Hope Holcomb was always frugal, stretching every penny for all it was worth. He grew up during the depression and experienced being without work and struggling just to have food to eat. It is no surprise that when Mama began sinking into the confusion of Alzheimer's that he cared for her at home; the struggle was considerable as she advanced from confusion, to rummaging through closets and cabinets, and finally wandering off several times.

Brent and I worried about Daddy, urging him to let us place Mama in a nursing home. He was already struggling to walk with two canes; it was too much for him to care for Mama alone. Finally, I confronted him, "Daddy, if you fell in the hall and broke your hip you could starve to death. Mama can't even call 911. As soon as she walked away she would forget you were there."

My harsh words made him pause and think, but still he insisted on caring for Mama alone. In less than two months Daddy fell and broke his shoulder; fortunately he was visiting relatives, and they cared for Mama as they awaited the ambulance. Still it was a difficult time for all of us. Daddy was immediately hospitalized for surgery, and Brent and I struggled from Columbia and Charlotte to arrange round the clock care for Mama throughout that fateful weekend. On Monday Mama was taken to a hospital and would soon be in a nursing home.

Daddy required several months of rehabilitation before returning to an empty house. We both had feared lacking the anchors of home would rob Mama of all memory of self and family. When we actually took her to the home, she surprised us both. Mama thought she worked there; she scurried about the ward, fluffing pillows and speaking to everyone. When she went behind the nurse's desk and began rifling papers, we tried to stop her. The nurses looked at us and calmly said, "Let her go. She can't hurt anything." At long last Mama was safe, well cared for, and happy. We could not have been more relieved.

Daddy insisted on living alone in that huge house. Even struggling with two canes, he managed to daily tend his garden. I feared he could fall and lay there for hours before anyone saw or heard him. But as Brent and I talked, we concluded that it gave Daddy happiness and provided needed exercise. Who were we to take away one of his few pleasures?

Daddy survived alone for a couple of years; he could still drive and went to church every Sunday. He frequently visited the video store where he would blow the horn and a clerk would come out and ask what he wanted. They came to know his tastes and stocked lots of old war movies just for him.

After two years Daddy was too unsteady to be safe alone and reluctantly agreed to move into assisted living. Mama was in a nursing home in Columbia where Brent visited her daily. But Daddy refused to leave Clinton, so every week Brent made the 60 mile trip to visit him. Once a month I drove 90 miles to Clinton and then took Daddy to Columbia to visit Mama. For one wonderful hour the whole family was reunited. When people asked why I would go to this effort, I replied "I could not live with my conscience if I didn't take the time to let them be together."

The long years of work caught up with Daddy very quickly. In just over two years his health declined and he required skilled care nursing, so we moved him to the same home with Mama. He was fading so fast. I remember the last time I saw him, completely bedridden. He asked me to raise the bed so he could talk with me. After only a couple of minutes he had to lie back down and was soon asleep. He was so pale, and his skin looked paper thin.

Creeping down the highway I didn't hold back the tears. "Lord, he is so frail. Please don't let it be long" I prayed aloud. In two days his breathing became very shallow, and he passed quietly.

But now I am drawn back into the present. Russel Dean, our pastor of many years, stands to give the eulogy. I turn to look behind me. I have never seen the church so full; every pew, even the balcony is filled - and a small crowd stands in the foyer as well.

Russel shares the many positions Daddy held at First Baptist - a deacon, an elder, an usher, an officer of the Men's Brotherhood, a speaker at many events always ready with an appropriate quotation from some long forgotten spokesperson. He was also a member of the Lion's Club, the Kiwanis, a Mason, and a Gideon. Daddy never preached or sang in the choir, but he did everything except unstop the toilets and work on the roof. During our childhood it seemed we were there every time the doors opened.

Gary Hope Holcomb barely completed high school. He met my mother, and when he was drafted for WWII, obtained a 3-day pass and they married. After the war he worked for a short while as a printer, but he longed to go into business for himself. He and Francis Blalock became partners and established a small business washing and pressing shirts. Mama and Daddy combined their money to buy a girl's bicycle to allow Daddy to ride to work even wearing a raincoat.

The business grew and expanded. By the time I was a teenager working there it was Sunshine Drycleaners and Laundry, with home delivery, a shoe repair shop, an alterations shop, 3 separate branch laundromats, and even uniform and tuxedo rental. My father and his partner operated the cleaners for 37 years before eventually selling the business to retire.

But far more important than his success as a businessman was my father's dedication as a Christian. He gave to the church, just how much I don't know. Every week my brother and I took 10% from our allowance and later from our earnings to put in our little envelopes to take to church. We were taught to take out the 10% before we spent anything for ourselves.

When I was still in grammar school the IRS contacted Daddy requiring him to appear for a personal audit. Daddy kept meticulous ledgers, and it was simple task for him to remove two books from his desk and report to the auditor. For hours the IRS agent inspected line after line and every check, finding accounting for every penny. At the end of the day the man told him, "Come back tomorrow. Bring the previous 7 years of records."

The following day went just as the first; the auditor could not find one item out of line. At the end of a long day of questions and waiting, the auditor replied that everything appeared to be correct and he was free to go. But Daddy was not about to leave without some explanation, so he asked, "Just what was it that you were looking for?"

In my imagination, I think the auditor must have blushed or stammered. "We just couldn't believe anyone actually gave that much to the church."

At one meeting of the Men's Brotherhood the speaker read poems they had written about their wives. All had been instructed to omit the names to see if the members could discern which spouse was being described. There was an outstanding humorous tale of a husband who came home from work and wanted to wash up but found every sink, the bathtub, and even the shower filled with flowers. Everyone laughed and knew Daddy was poking good-natured fun at Mama's passion for floral arranging.

During my first two years of college I had studied to become a minister; finally I concluded I had misjudged God's direction and changed majors. Daddy sat down with me and we discussed the reasons for my decision. It was then that he revealed that he, too, had once felt called to the ministry.

Brent and I were small children at the time. Daddy had felt so compelled that he even applied and was accepted at seminary. He laid a fleece before the Lord, to be certain he was following the correct leading. But the finances never materialized. He sadly shared with me that his conclusion was "many are called, but few are chosen."

For years he still felt that longing within him. After retirement with enthusiasm Daddy attended Fourth Division reunions, mingling again with soldiers he had known during WWII. His faith was so evident that they unanimously voted making him an honorary chaplain. Daddy was thrilled to the core of his being; he wrote and printed books of devotions and prayers which he mailed to many of his army friends. His long desire was finally fulfilled.

And Russel shared a story I had never heard before. At the time the church was meeting in the Hampton Street School while the new sanctuary was being built; during a congregational meeting it was suggested that the church should purchase a new organ. As Brent was already studying piano and organ, this was an issue which touched Daddy's heart.

One after another members stood to express their views. Many suggested that the church was already in too much debt with the construction underway; it was unwise to take on another huge expense. Others stood stating the old organ was beyond repair and replacement was absolutely necessary. Some suggested a cheap organ as a temporary solution. There were strong heated opinions, and the opposing sides were becoming entrenched.

Daddy was a man of few but clear words. When the group grew quiet, he stood to give his voice. He stated that the Lord was great, and if we were to worship Him in a new sanctuary that we also needed a magnificent organ to praise Him. "I believe that we SHOULD purchase a new organ, and I want to be the first to give twenty dollars to the fund." Twenty dollars was a great deal of money at that time. Daddy stepped forward and placed the bill in the offering plate.

His bold action began a flood, and there was no stemming the tide. One after another stood and walked to the front placing money in the plate, establishing firmly the New Organ Fund. That fund purchased the same organ we heard at the beginning of this service.

Russel went on to compare Daddy to a guard, a soldier in God's army. Daddy was but one of many men of similar character; the names J D McKee, George Corley, Judson Brehmer, and Rembert Truluck immediately come to my mind. All of them have passed, and are there are others coming up to take their places? I am sorry, but I see very few. Faithfulness and devotion seemed to be much more common in that generation.

I look back with great affection and respect for my father. Often I hear myself saying, "My Daddy always said . . . " or "I wish I had half the business sense my father had." Each time my brother and I meet, we always end up talking about him. I had a wonderful father, a genuine saint who gave me a legacy of memories and faith. I am determined to be one of the guards to replace him. I hope when I am gone my children will look back on my life with the same respect that I have towards my father. Truly, he was a member of the guard.

CHAPTER 4

Michael

Not Your Usual Tourist

Last year I spent a few short days on the coast that forever changed my outlook on vacations. Originally I planned the usual beach trip. I would walk the beach, build a sandcastle, play putt-putt, and buy a tacky t-shirt.

Much had happened in the two years previous. After Carol passed away, we moved to a smaller house. Now Nathan was out on his own, and Adria was about to depart for college. Venturing onto the internet, I began searching for new interests and friends. Art of all kinds and photography had always interested me, so it was natural that I made friends with Michael Brooks, who was both a nature photographer and 3D artist.

Having not visited the beach for several years, I was eager to enjoy the sun, salt and sand again. Not wanting to go alone, I asked my Michael if he would like to come along. He volunteered to accompany me and transform the trip into a wildlife and nature shoot.

We arrived late that night at Shallotte and the following morning made the trek to Ocean Isle before sunrise. Crossing the high-rise bridge, I scanned the crowded rows of houses facing the deep blue water rushing toward the sand. Excitement began to rise within me.

As Michael pulled cameras and tripod out of the trunk, I scanned the sky. The salt air and gentle roar of the surf stirred my senses, and the longing for the ocean surged within me. I rushed towards the beach to find the first rays of the sun were peeking over the horizon. A red glow filled the sky and fiery white traced the outlines of the clouds.

I stood mesmerized, captured by the sights, smells, and sounds as Michael stood yelling for help to unload the equipment. Finally I snapped back to the present, reluctantly turning my back to sun, but momentarily we were both watching the sun play hide and seek through the clouds, changing color by the split-second. We snapped one picture after another capturing the progress toward full day. Much later when we repacked the car, I noticed it was actually quite cold.

When we returned that afternoon the sun teased us even more with setting than rising. The clouds descended like a window shade, blocking much of the yellow ball. Again, we had a beautiful view, but not all we had anticipated.

Thursday we slept in, resting for an afternoon shoot. Michael had permission to visit a private lake where we could photograph aquatic birds. After wending our way through a maze of backroads, we arrived at a trailer tucked under a canopy of trees draped with Spanish moss.

We entered the home and visited briefly with Donnie, who pointed proudly to framed photos Michael had taken here years ago. We quickly said our thanks and exited to begin our safari. We trekked a dirt road nearly a mile to a bank which yielded a clear view of the secluded lake.

My first attempt to photograph a passing heron sent Michael into a fit of anger followed by uncontrollable laughter. Crouched behind my cover, I waited for the bird to glide close overhead. Suddenly I popped up like a slice of bread from a toaster, expecting to capture a fantastic shot. Instead I startled the bird who rocketed away. Michael quickly taught me to select a better spot from which I could shoot without changing position and alerting half the wildlife in the county.

The majority of the afternoon we saw and heard no one. An old pickup truck rattled down the road behind us and then stopped; the driver had spotted us in the undergrowth and was curious about these strangers on Donnie's private land. After performing his background check, he warned us to "watch out for them gators." Michael wasn't surprised, but my eyes grew to the size of saucers. "They's several gators, but Ralph, now he's the one to watch out fer. He's 12 foot long, not counting the tail."

Before climbing back up the bank, he pointed out Ralph's favorite sunning spot, reminding us several times Ralph was 12 foot long, not counting the tail.

I discovered photographing wildlife is much like fishing. Years before I often fished with my father and brother. I recall long periods of waiting, sitting quietly, watching for the cork to bob. Eventually I'd snag a fish with my pole. After several moments of excitement pulling my catch from the water, I would put the fish away and return to the quiet waiting.

Over the years I have associated fishing with relaxation and peace, a complete retreat from the world. Such were my feelings this afternoon - long periods of quiet expectation - followed by a short thrill when a crane or ibis flew close overhead. If we were quick, we would catch the bird on film. If we failed to react in time, we experienced a short disappointment, followed by more waiting.

We waited and watched, enjoying the sights whether we captured them or not. Several times a frog jumped and splashed right in front of us; each time we jumped, ready to run in case Ralph had decided to pay us a visit. The afternoon of birds and biting bugs was drawing to a close. We repacked and said our thanks, dashing back to Ocean Isle to capture the sunset. Bright slices of sun, passing through thin strips of clouds, displayed shades of orange, red, and purple. Sparkling shots of shimmering reflections on the waves were our treasures of the day.

Friday, rising before daylight, Michael hoped to catch ol' sol making a brilliant entrance. On the shore, chill air and sounds of the surf breaking on the sand accompanied the bursting sunrise. The sun rose in clear glory - no clouds obstructed a single ray of his radiance. My skill had grown since our first morning. Michael could now ask me for a particular lens or filter or a different speed of film. And I didn't leave him stranded when I saw a beautiful scene like the first morning.

Afterwards we visited C.W.'s Grill for a light breakfast and a full plate of conversation. Allyson Hughes operated the grill for years and had been like a second mother to Michael and other school kids. She was delighted to see him. He rose in respect, pulling out a chair for her. Her hair was silver now, and she moved much slower than he remembered. She squinted to see his photos, so he found a magnifier. I saw a kindness and affection between them you don't see often nowadays, especially between generations. Together they browsed photos from the past and caught up on the lives of old friends.

That afternoon we returned to Donnie's property; on one side was the lake, but a mile back, we had a view of Shallotte Point across the intercoastal waterway. Today we shared a better sense of the birds' movements; they flew from one bank to another, following the warmth of the climbing sun. Anticipating their moves, we were better prepared to capture their flights.

We positioned our cameras to face the waterway and capture the sun descending behind Shallotte Point. We shared a growing suspicion the view here would be spectacular.

We grew anxious, scrutinizing the sky during the countdown to the descent. And then, the sun began to paint the clouds, all the dabs and highlights reflected on the water below. Myriad shades and splashes in the clouds were presented in dual vision. Using several cameras, we changed positions and angles, racing to capture as many shots as possible before the sky grew dark. Without a doubt, this final photo session had been our best.

Saturday we reluctantly abandoned the coast. I returned refreshed by my vacation, not weary and exhausted. I had not been the usual tourist nor had I experienced the usual vacation. But just as if I had been fishing, I had tall tales of the one that got away, and I had trophies to hang on my wall. Instead of a mounted carp, I have beautiful images of God's handiwork, displaying the beauty He had unveiled.

I am looking forward to another vacation early next year and another wildlife shoot. I don't think I will ever be the usual tourist again.

Not Just a Dog

Michael gets down on his knees, examining the dog's oozing wounds, treating them tenderly and delicately. His touch is akin to that of a surgeon or maybe an angel.

When Michael was in his twenties, without much education, he lived alone with Gene, who worked landscaping and odd jobs, Michael assisting him most of the time. But when Michael's seizures increased, Gene took him to a dog breeder, telling him to choose a puppy. Michael selected a Dalmatian, the most alert from the litter, immediately naming her Turba Girl. Never since has he received a better gift.

When she was small, she never left his side. He would tuck her inside his shirt where she snuggled up and napped against his warm belly. Even while landscaping or visiting the grocery store, no one suspected she was there.

Turba soon grew too large to go on jobs with Michael, but at home she waited patiently. At the first rattle of Gene's old pickup, she wagged her tail and paced excitedly, anxious to see her master again.

No one knows what instinct taught her about seizures, but she quickly learned what they were and recognized their approach. If she sensed a seizure was imminent, an army could not have dragged her away from Michael. When he fell to the floor, she tugged at his sleeve and nipped his hand, attempting to awake him. When she could not, she laid her head on his chest, waiting for him to return to consciousness. At the first flutter of his eyelids, she would yip and lick his face. She stayed right there, wagging her tail and licking until he could sit up and speak to her.

A few years later Gene passed away, leaving Michael alone with only Turba to watch over him. Michael could not drive because of his seizures, and employers were reluctant to hire an epileptic, fearing the event of an injury. Fortunately, Gene had planned ahead and a few weeks after his death, Michael received his first disability check. It wasn't much, but it could pay rent and utilities; if Michael really pinched pennies, he could buy groceries for the month.

Every day Turba stayed by his side. She would chase the frisbee he tossed, catching and fetching until she panted with thirst. Turba was not just a pet; she was his family as surely as if she were his child. Michael talked with her and confided in her as a trusted friend. She listened and trusted him completely.

On the rare occasions when Michael ate at McDonald's or at a friend's home, he always saved a bite and brought it home to Turba. She relished it as though it was the finest sirloin. They walked together, ate together, watched television together, slept together. In the winter she curled up at his back and kept him warm. In the summer, she slept at his feet.

From time to time she had minor injuries and ailments, as any animal will. Michael cared for scrapes, insect bites, and thorns. Turba did not enjoy these treatments, but she trusted Michael. If she stepped on a thorn, she immediately limped to him, begging his help. Even if a wound was tender and painful, she did not resist his care, though she lay trembling.

But now, Turba has come on more difficult times. She is nearly 13 years old. Arthritis has affected her joints, and she moves slowly down the three steps to the yard. Turba and Michael used to share long walks far from home, but now just a short walk around the yard takes her breath away. She never had a problem before, but now sometimes she wets the floor at night. Turba still wags her tail at the sound of his voice, but every day it appears to take her longer to stand up and to lie down.

And now, a new problem has arisen, and it requires all of Michael's love and skill to care for her. First, a large ugly ulcer appeared on her paw. He washed it, applied ointment, and carefully wrapped it day after day. But it didn't improve. And then, another appeared on her back. It, too, resisted all his careful attentions. Then three more appeared on her belly.

He sought advice from other dog owners and tried every home remedy he could find. But the condition grew steadily worse. Not only did he lack funds to take her to a vet, but he feared the news it would reveal. Michael now lives with me instead of a ramshackle trailer. I volunteered to take Turba to the vet and help pay the bill.

And now, his worst fear has come upon him. His companion, his child and confidante, has Cushion's Disease. In a younger, stronger dog treatment might extend life. Turba's age and weight have made the condition more serious. She doesn't have much time, a month or two, maybe less.

Herein lies the pain of this gentle soul; the heart which beats in rhythm to his own will soon beat no longer. In love, he will care for her and ease her pain, but soon her life will cease to be happy. When that time comes, he will not allow her to suffer. He will use his meager funds and take her to the vet, where she can lie down and sleep under his gentle caress.

She has spent her entire life attending to him and loving him. And soon, because of his love for her, he will help her die gently and quietly.

She is a friend, a child, a bringer of comfort and happiness to an otherwise lonely life. This gentle beast was a gift, not just a gift from a person; she was a gift from God.

Less than a week has passed, and things have taken a change for the worse. When Michael let Turba out to the front yard, she descended the steps even slower than usual. In a few minutes, she stood on the first step wanting to re-enter. She waited to gather the strength to climb the steps, and finally when the strength failed to come, she lay down shivering in the cold wet grass.

Michael gently lifted her and brought her into the house. I petted and comforted Turba as he called the vet and his mother. Together we carefully placed Turba on a blanket in the backseat. Michael rode with her, holding her and talking to her. She sat up, enjoying the ride and the breeze. She hadn't been able to ride for some time. She licked Michael's face.

The staff at the Dr. James' office were kind and understanding; Michael waited in the car with Turba until Dr. James came and spoke with him. Together we gently placed Turba on an outside table. This remarkable vet looked with empathy at Michael and softly said, "You are doing the right thing. It's her time."

He gently trimmed a small amount of hair from a foreleg, preparing it for the injection. And as Michael stroked her and told her goodbye, her eyes began to cloud, and she lay her head down and slept.

After a few minutes we drove to his mother's home; she had invited Michael to bury Turba there, where she used to play. Michael wrapped her in her favorite blanket and buried her on the edge of the field where she caught the frisbee and chased rabbits.

Michael wept without shame, thanking Turba for all she had done for him and telling her he was sorry he couldn't make her well. He stood there for a long time before he picked some wildflowers and left them on her grave.

A Gift from Heaven

Only two days earlier, Michael and I had driven to Salisbury and laid his dear Turba to rest. He wept frequently and was so lonely without her.

It pained me to see him so distraught and alone; he had long hours alone while I worked.

His eyes bleary and red, Michael asked me softly, "Do you think it's too soon to get another dog?"

I chose my words carefully. "Only you can decide if it's too soon, Michael. But if you feel ready, I certainly don't mind if you get another dog." We talked about how loving Turba had been, but I did point out that

Dalmatians are prone to skin, vision, and hearing problems. He felt, however, his next companion HAD to be a Dalmatian and HAD to be female.

"Ok, I'll start searching the web now," I replied as he withdrew to his computer. I searched for breeders for quite some time, but it seemed they were all distant and very expensive. I even made several calls without any luck. I whispered under my breath "Lord, I need some help with this."

Suddenly, I remembered that I had once met the president of The Charlotte Kennel Cub, and I kept her business card. In moments she and I were speaking on the phone. She stated she knew several kennels in the area which bred Dalmatians and that she would gladly email me a list.

It was almost time to depart for work, and I hadn't heard anything. Michael asked, "Would you check one more time before you go?"

There it was. I opened her email and saw a long list of breeders in the area. But at the last second she had added a note. "I just got a call from a Mrs. Porter in Matthews; she found an abandoned puppy covered in mud. She took it to the vet and paid for the inoculations. The vet told her it's a full-blooded Dalmatian. She needs to find it a home and only wants to be reimbursed for the vet bill."

I hollered for Michael. "Read this and tell me Someone isn't watching over you," I said, pointing to the letter on my screen. He read it over my shoulder.

"Call her, call her!" he exclaimed.

In just a minute I was chatting with Mrs. Porter. Yes, she still had the puppy, yes, the puppy had all necessary shots. She only wanted reimbursement, $77 for the vet bill. Could we come and see the pup tomorrow? Yes, midmorning about 9:30 would be fine. Fidgeting excitedly beside me, Michael prompted me with one final question. Yes, the pup is female.

I thanked her and put down the phone. Michael was almost in tears.

The next morning as I sipped my first coffee at 6:15, Michael stumbled into my office. I peered over the rim of my cup at him standing in his underwear. "I'm ready. Can we go now?"

He was both excited and apprehensive, like a boy on his first date. "What if she doesn't like me?" he asked.

As I followed the directions, I noticed the houses were getting larger and larger. I found myself driving through a million dollar neighborhood. I cautiously approached the address. My little car looked lost in the driveway.

Mrs. Porter was gracious, chatting as she took us to meet the pup. The little one was skittish at first, but Michael gently took her into his arms. They soon locked eyes, and the pup licked his face. They were already bonding.

As she saw them becoming attached, Mrs. Porter turned and asked me, "You DO have a fenced yard, don't you?" I explained that my backyard was fenced, and the pup would have all the running space, fresh air and sunshine she needed. Mrs. Porter already had no doubts about the love Michael would bestow upon her. I paid her and we headed towards home.

On the drive, Michael named the pup Furba Girl, in memory of Turba and with the hope that she would have similar qualities. To me, it already appeared that she had Turba's gentle temperament. At home I examined a photo of Turba and checked out a suspicion I had. Furba has a pattern of four spots on her crown almost identical to Turba.

Late that night, Michael suffered two *grand mal* seizures. But Furba did not run from him; she possessed the same instinct as Turba, somehow understanding this is an affliction. She would not leave his side. Furba watched every breath until he returned to consciousness, and then she showed her concern and love by licking his face. The following morning I noticed a change in her behavior, now protective and possessive of her new master. The entire day she never ventured more than two feet from his side.

Michael's *grand mals* typically come in clusters of three. The third waited several days before making its appearance; the onset was sudden, not even affording the usual courtesy of a few moments warning. Michael was walking down the hall when he suddenly started flailing his arms, smashing two large pictures and sending a shower of glass in every direction. Now on the floor, his arms twitched and his feet kicked as he lay unconscious. Furba lay curled up on his chest. I feared both of they might be cut and tried to approach; shards of glass in my palms and my knees forced me to withdraw, but I could not find a scratch or even a splinter on Michael or Furba.

These events bring a Bible verse to my mind - AND IT SHALL COME TO PASS, THAT BEFORE THEY CALL, I WILL ANSWER; AND WHILE THEY ARE YET SPEAK-ING, I WILL HEAR. Before I had even begun searching and praying, God had orchestrated a magnificent answer.

Several months later when booster shots were due, we returned to the vet. For reference I asked the vet to record Furba's estimated birth-date. Upon returning home, I tossed the papers in a drawer. Months later I reviewed the documents, and one more detail was revealed. Furba was born on Michael's birthday, a literal gift from heaven.

Furba appears to be growing by the minute, and Michael looks and acts 10 years younger. Furba has not replaced Turba in our hearts, but she has come to fulfill her role of attendant and protector. If I didn't know better, I would say Turba was standing close by instructing little Furba.

Strangle that Bird!

Gail and Michael were best friends during high school days, so when she purchased a digital camera, we gladly accepted the invitation to visit. They could catch up on old times, and Michael would help hone her photographic skill. Michael and Gail marched through the woods in search of wildlife; afterward we went to the beach, where they tested her skill shooting waves and the sunset.

That evening we relaxed, chatting until well after midnight. Her sister Ethel Mae joined us, proudly displaying the talents of Sunshine, her pet cockatiel. The bird could say a few words and gleefully whistled several tunes. During any pause in the conversation, Sunshine would strike up a happy little song. She whistled *Mary Had a Little Lamb, Jingle Bells* and *Jesus Loves Me*.

Finally all agreed it was time for a night's rest. As the ladies retreated to their bedrooms, Michael spread out covers on the sofa while I made a pallet on floor. Stretching and yawning, we felt the sleep dragging us away.

But a spring in the sofa gave Michael a sharp jab; he adjusted the covers and turned over. Then another poked him in the shoulder. Reversing position to the opposite end of the sofa, he added another blanket. Finally he was comfortable. The tossing and turning was over, and we began drifting into peaceful slumber. That's when it all started. In her cage behind the sofa, Sunshine decided it was time for a song.

First she whistled *Mary Had a Little Lamb*. I breathed a heavy sigh and my wide-open eyes slowly returned to half-mast. Sharp tones again pierced the darkness as Sunshine whistled *Jingle Bells*, twice. As Michael grumbled words best not repeated, I crossed my fingers and held my breath, wishing that little feathered hellion would shut up.

But then Sunshine had the bright idea to whistle *Pop Goes the Weasel*. I'm sure you remember the little ditty we sang in kindergarten.

Round and round the mulberry bush,
the monkey chased the weasel.
The monkey thought twas all in fun.
POP! goes the weasel.

If Sunshine had whistled it once and finished, all would have been fine. But the silly bird couldn't remember the end. She whistled the first three lines and stopped.

She paused, trying in vain to recall the missing notes. After a minute she started again. I don't know how many times that stupid bird repeated the little rhyme. Over and over I hoped Sunshine would complete the song and return to silence.

Again she reached the upbeat and paused. Grinding my teeth with frustration, I listened anxiously expecting the final verse. I heard Michael tossing back and forth, angry enough to spit. I half expected him to jump up and throw the cage out the door. I, too, was approaching an explosion.

Here it came again. Michael sprang upright and grabbed the sides of the cage. "Pop goes the weasel, dammit! Pop goes the weasel! Can't you remember that, you stupid little bird???!!!!"

By the moonlight shining through the curtains, I could see everything. Sunshine looked at him from her little perch, completely unafraid. She blinked those little black eyes and cocked her head sideways as if studying him. Howls of laughter echoed up the hall from the sisters' bedrooms.

Sunshine made not a peep. Michael lay back down, and I adjusted the covers and slowly reclined. Sleep - at last.

And then, another whistle. "Pop! Goes the weasel" Sunshine sang. She whistled it again, "Pop! Goes the weasel."

Sunshine continued chirping that one line most of the night. Eventually I faded into a troubled sleep, punctuated with dreams of exploding weasels and screeching yellow birds.

What Good is an Old Grouch?

He mutters under his breath as he squints into the viewfinder, adjusting aperture and film speed for the darkness. Next door a mysterious car has arrived. He zooms in, capturing images of money changing hands, a small package slipped from one person to another, someone lighting up an illegal substance, and the license plate. He will snap many photos over the next few months, shooting from behind a curtain in the late night hours.

Another night he dons camouflage and squats behind the bushes at 1:00 AM. He shivers through cold and drizzling rain, capturing more license plates to report to the police. He whispers to himself, fighting the urge to scream out at the dope peddlers.

Yes, he's an old grouch. He generally keeps to himself, minding his own business. But he hates seeing illegal activities infiltrating this neighborhood of quiet retirees, widows, and parents with young children. People have become afraid to walk down the street; no one lets their children play outside anymore.

There's much more than meets the eye of this old grouch. If you knock on his door selling some product, you won't be there long. And don't make the mistake of calling him for a survey. His blistering response will burn your ears and you will hang up hastily.

You might say his belligerent attitude stems from years of abuse as a child, or it could be his reaction to years of prejudice. His father believed that the diagnosis of epilepsy meant he was mentally retarded. He attempted to surrender his own son to an institution and treated him like the scum of the earth. When Michael could bear the abuse no longer, he ran away. He chose life on the streets as preferable to the mental and physical anguish he had endured.

But Michael Brooks is far more than just a grouch with a sharp tongue. He is a believer, but you probably won't see him in church. He prays daily, asking for protection and guidance and thanking God for His help in many ways. But people with good intentions ask questions uncomfortable for him to answer, like why doesn't he work, what kind of disability does he have, or why isn't he married. That discomfort and the fear of having a seizure in public are enough to keep him to himself. It may surprise you to learn that God watches over him in mysterious ways.

When he was still living on the streets, God sent an angel in the form of a retired Army sergeant who took him in and sought medical attention for his seizures. This man taught him about life and a trade, photography.

Later God sent him another companion, a Dalmatian puppy. This loving dog could sense impending seizures and stayed by his side, guarding him whenever he was afflicted. After the sergeant passed away, he had only this loving Dalmatian but, with her by his side, he developed his skills further, photographing nature and creating works of art. He sought out beauty to help him forget his past, and he shared the beauty he found.

And when after years of faithful service, his loving dog had to be put to sleep, God showed him amazing favor again. Within three days an abandoned Dalmatian puppy was given to him. She too possessed the amazing instincts concerning seizures and immediately became his new companion and guardian. And when the vet examined her and estimated her date of birth, Michael saw another sign of God's hand. She was born on his birthday.

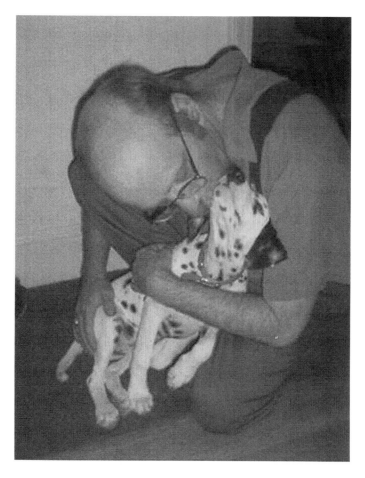

Last year Michael became even moodier than usual; those close to him knew something was wrong. But even though he was suffering constant abdominal pain, seizures, digestive and kidney problems, he still thought of others. He donated artworks to churches and to the Kidney Foundation, and he raised funds to help an artist in California diagnosed with terminal cancer. He undertook involved plans to raise funds for a small community volunteer fire department.

He despises going to the doctor, always has. He hates being labeled, probed and poked, diagnosed, and examined. Only after prolonged pain did he finally consent to an examination, and for some time the treatments only multiplied the problems. Eventually doctors determined that two medications were in conflict and were creating physical stress and pain. Slowly he began to mend and his better instincts came back to the forefront. Now he is undergoing treatment for a liver condition which eventually will end his life.

But he does have friends - people who love this old grouch. They see beyond his rough exterior to the kind and giving heart beneath. That's why people around the globe worked together to create a surprise birthday party for this man. They returned his friendship with photographs, art and music, things he loves.

Emails, cards, letters, photos, poems, video clips and songs were sent from as far away as England, South Africa, Washington, Canada - from various ages and ethnic groups - to cheer this old grouch. He was honored with a special video and a scrapbook containing remembrances from some of those his work has touched. The walls were decorated with articles about him and examples of his photos in papers and magazines. A speech was given in his honor and he was presented with certificates and honor befitting his hidden nature. A reporter was present, later telling his story on the front page of the local paper.

Of course, he fussed and fumed about the whole thing. He grumbled and muttered when they all yelled "surprise!" But he really appreciated it. He was moved that people care about him and appreciate his friendship.

What happened to the neighbors? Michael is not a big man - only 5 foot 4. But when I saw him threatened by a huge man from the house next door, Michael defiantly stood his ground. He had no weapon but the camera around his neck. Eventually his evidence did the trick; a SWAT team broke down the door of that house, carrying everyone in it away. Several neighbors came and thanked him. The following day I saw an elderly couple walking down the street together and a young mother pushing her child in a stroller.

So, what good is an old grouch? There is actually a lot of good in this one - good purpose, good intentions, and a great big heart.

The View from 12 Inches High

Hi. I'm Dee Dee. I sure am glad you speak Dog; most people can't speak with me.

Right now I am waiting. Barry has taken Furba for her morning walk, and then comes my turn. I sit right here watching the door till they return. Furba is a Dalmatian; my breed is Old Black Mutt. Barry says I am solid black except where I turned gray around my muzzle. I can't see it, but I guess he's right.

Here they come up the street now. He stops at the edge of the yard and removes her leash. She won't step one paw outside the yard without him. He knows me better than that; he makes me wear a harness because I can slip out of any collar.

He opens the door and I jump up and down, telling him I am ready. Sometimes he says "wait a minute," and gets a drink or goes to the bathroom. If he hangs up his sweater, I'll have to wait even longer. He might have a cup of coffee or turn on the talking-picture-box. Each time I nudge his hand to remind him, he says, "just a minute." Sometimes he says it so many times I growl to tell him I REALLY want to go.

Now he is holding the harness. I stand still as he puts it over my head and fastens the strap around my belly. With a little time I could figure out how to get out of this thing, but as soon as we return, he hangs it up till tomorrow.

We stand on the porch and pause. I let out three loud barks to tell the neighborhood, "This is MY house and MY person. You stay away from here!" Now we can go.

I stop to sniff the lamp post at the edge of the yard. Damn! Some dog has been here and left his mark. I've gotta cover that up.

Now we cross the street. Oh Boy! Lots of trees and bushes to sniff. This is almost as fun as chew-chew time. Barry holds the leash tight and won't let me pull him; he will yank and make me walk at his speed. And he always makes me walk on the grass while he walks in the street where he can see the cars coming. He used to say something about "left, Dee Dee. Stay on the left." I don't know what that meant, but he always makes me walk on this side.

My first people weren't nice to me; they chained me to a tree, and I never had enough food or water. Sometimes they hit me with a stick. One back leg still hurts when it gets cold, and it makes me limp. When I got loose, I ran far away and never went back. Michael's Mama was driving and saw me by the road; Michael put me in the car and took me home with them. I was starving, and I was covered with ticks and fleas. But Michael cleaned me up real good and fed me and petted me. He talked to me a lot and taught me some People words. I learned to love his Mama and stayed by her feet every day; I growled at anyone I didn't know who tried to get close to her.

But Mama had to go to the hospital for something they called cat-a-rax; you know anything coming from cats is bad. Mama hugged me and said she was afraid she would trip over me; that's when I came to live with Michael and Barry. Mama comes to visit some times, and I snuggle up next to her feet like old times.

Over there's a beer can; I know what those are and can smell it from here. Up ahead I see a paper bag; that should be interesting. But he won't let me tear it open to see if there is any food left in it.

I am anxious to get to the corner and check out the Dog Bulletin Board. All the dogs stop and leave their calling card here. I like to take a minute and smell ALL the markers. If we meet another dog out on a walk, I will already know him.

Barry says "Wait!" and I sit. Either cars are coming, or he is looking at some flowers. When he says, "OK," then we will cross the street. There's a huge dog inside that tall fence near the corner. I think Barry said his breed is Mongrel; no, he said Mangy Mongrel. He already smells me and runs back and forth, barking and leaping against the fence. He sounds tough, but he doesn't scare me. I growl low and deep, letting him see the fur stand on my back. I look straight at him while I squat and drop a pile so he can remember me. It drives him nuts. I scratch the grass to cover it just a bit and strut proudly away, never looking back.

We walk another block before we cross the street and turn. There's a cat on that porch; I jerk like I could charge and chase him, but Barry won't loosen his grip. I just like to see the cat crouch ready to run.

Barry and Michael actually have two cats; how disgusting. They come and go, in and out, never on a leash. They can eat anytime, but our chew-chew times are only in the morning and the evening. Furba and I always leave a little bit in our bowls; we may come back to nibble, but mostly it's for fun. We watch for a cat to get close to a bowl, and when they do, we bark and chase them down the hall. We've got to show them who's boss every now and then.

Yesterday we got a surprise. Barry called us, and in each hand he held a steak bone. Furba trotted to her corner, and I went to mine; then we could enjoy our juicy treats. Furba never has learned to make her bone last like I do. She gnaws and crunches and finishes her bone in just a little while. I take my time, licking and gnawing while she stares at me, wishing she still had hers. She has tried before, but Barry won't let her take mine. If she does, he will take it back and shut her in the bedroom in the dark. She whines when she's left alone.

Later, when he sends us outside to do business, I still have my bone. I carry it in my mouth because she is just waiting for me to put it down. Soon he calls, and Furba hurries back into the house. He looks at me and calls again, but I'm not going. I turn my back and sit. He closes the door and leaves me to bury my bone, but I still have to outsmart Furba or she will find it. I make extra holes all around the yard, nosing in a few leaves and covering them; our next time out she will go from hole to hole, searching for my bone. I watch her digging everywhere, while I sit quietly, right on top of my bone. Furba is still like a pup; she'll figure it out one day.

Down the street we go, past houses, trees and bushes, and all of them have been marked. Barry walks on steadily, only letting me stop and sniff occasionally. He usually slows down and looks here; that lady spends a lot of time working in her yard. I always like going by that one; there are two Chihuahuas inside, and they have a fit when we walk by. They jump up and down yappity-yapping the whole time; I always leave a marker right while they are watching.

Most of the time we don't meet other dogs; Barry stays on his side of the street, and others pass on the opposite side. I always bark before they get close, warning them this is MY person and to stay away. But to-day Barry sees John walking with Solomon. He is much bigger than me; he's a Husky. But we are friends just like Barry and John; they stand and talk while Solomon and I sniff and wag together. When they finish talking, Solomon and John go back across the street. Solomon is strong and drags John from one side of the street to the other.

I see my house up ahead. I slow down just a bit, getting in a few more sniffs and leaving another marker or two on the bushes. I want all the dogs to know this is MY street.

Barry won't remove the harness until the door is closed. He remem-bers when I ran off a few years ago. I was gone for three days, chasing rab-bits and sniffing garbage cans for blocks. I found a dead squirrel - and Oh, what a smell it was! I rolled and rolled in it to bring back that wonderful scent. It was like all of outdoors.

But when I returned, Barry was not happy with me at all; he held his nose and took me straight to the tub. He scrubbed me and washed me un-til all my wonderful perfume was gone. I sulked in the corner for two days.

We're back in the house now. Barry sits on the sofa and turns on the talking-picture-box. Michael comes out of his room and asks me where I've been and scratches me behind the ears. He speaks very fluent Dog and always knows what I like.

Once in a while Barry and Michael take us to ride in the car; Furba sticks her head out the window enjoying the wind blowing her face. I like the fresh air and all the wonderful scents, but I am content with the breeze coming through the window. If it's a long ride, we may visit a Magic Window; they are fabulous. Barry pulls the car up to a box and talks to it; then he drives to the window and food comes out. It's magic! Furba will stick her head out and wag her tail; sometimes they give Barry little biscuits for us.

Barry put up that sparkly tree again a few days ago; I know what that means. Soon there will be boxes under it - boxes I am not allowed to sniff.

One day Barry will cook a long time in the kitchen; Furba and I will sit and watch, hoping he will spill something tasty. Eventually he will drop just two little bites, one for each of us; then he will send us out of the kitchen. That day his children will come and open the boxes; everyone will get a big red sock with treats in it. Furba and I will get snacks and maybe a bone out of a red sock, too. That night, when Michael and Barry eat again, they might let us lick the plates.

It's been a fun day; I went on a long walk and got to say "Hi" to Solomon, and soon we will get something from a red sock. It's a good life.

I can't wait till tomorrow to go walking again.

Time, Precious Time

I never thought it would end like this. I thought we would grow old together, laughing through rocking chair races and helping each other up from the sofa. But today I saw that faraway look in his eyes. Waking from a nap he looked around his room, not sure where he was or who I am. In a minute, he came groggily back to the present.

It was only 10 years ago when we met. I was a 45-year-old widower with too much time on my hands. Michael was a disabled photographer, existing in a tiny trailer in the middle of nowhere. Soon he was teaching me photography and computer graphics. I was making frequent visits to transport him to the grocery store and to the pharmacy for his epilepsy medications. Soon it made more sense for him to move in with me. I wouldn't be lonely, and he would have easy access to groceries, doctors and pharmacies.

The first couple of years were hysterical – me learning the guts of computers and the finer points of graphics programs; Michael learning about credit, contracts, commissions and what NOT to say to potential buyers. When a CD of graphics was rejected, I asked him to show me the submission letter. Reading it, I was appalled at the grammar and lack of order. I made him promise to never write another business letter again and to let me do all his correspondence. I rewrote the letter with an apology, asking them to take a second look at the graphics. They bought 80% of the images.

It was a strange partnership, but somehow it worked. I was gentle, polite, and patient; he was crusty, cussing and hotheaded. Michael took the photos and made the graphics. I found the buyers and negotiated the contracts. He was soon making more money than he had in a long time, and I was enjoying working on computers and even making a few dollars restoring photos.

We made trips and visited friends on the coast. It seemed everyone knew Michael and welcomed him into their homes. We tramped through woods, over hills, capturing photos of sunsets and coastal wildlife.

Then peculiar health problems began to arise. The doctor changed his seizure medication, and he became so moody and irritable that he lost most of his friends. He suffered constant abdominal and joint pain, losing weight until he was just a shadow of his former self. Our relationship became strained as he argued and complained. Michael realized what was happening and begged a week away at the coast with a few remaining friends. Before three days passed, they called begging me to take him to his doctor. I rushed through the four-hour drive there and back, alerting the doctor's office we were coming. He was groaning and near collapse as I lifted him onto the examining table. Blinded by my tears, I urged the doctor, "HELP HIM!"

Gradually, medication changes brought some relief. The abdominal pains subsided, and his weight slowly returned, but depression took hold as he found himself terribly alone. Friends would not be won back. Phone calls and letters were unanswered, and contracts had been lost. During my long hours of work he was at home alone, and despair closed in around him.

Then even more bad news slapped him in the face. He was diagnosed with advanced hepatitis C and resulting cirrhosis of the liver. We went to specialist after specialist, but the news was not good. Epilepsy and other conditions prevented him from receiving the only medication used to treat his liver disease. All we could do was wait for the inevitable, trying to make the best of life while it lasted.

Over the next year, we made more trips to the coast, spending time with the few remaining friends. But soon, the effects of the his illness made travel impractical. He tired so easily and slept so long after any exertion. He used to watch movies and play video games until late in the night; now he had little interest in his former pleasures. And the pain in his belly never completely went away. The joint pains returned with a vengeance, making even quick excursions to the store nearly unbearable.

Gradually, I noticed a new problem. Ever since I had known him, Michael had a detailed knowledge of his computers, programs and video games, searching through hundreds of files and disks with ease. Now, he was having difficulty with even simple tasks on the computer, and he struggled to play some of his favorite games.

God, in His infinite Wisdom, sometimes introduces unexpected blessings. When my daughter called to tell me she and her husband were making me a grandfather, I was thrilled with the news, but later wondered how this would affect Michael. He had always liked children, but now noise made him irritable. He loved my daughter, but would a baby's cries cause him to withdraw from her visits? All my fears were for naught, because when my grandson finally arrived, Michael fell in love with Giovany. The cries of a baby didn't worry him, and when the parents chose him as Godfather, he was speechless with the honor. On his own initiative, he dug out his forgotten cameras to take photos and movies of his little godson. Michael was the guest of honor at Giovany's first birthday.

Christmas had never been an important holiday to Michael, but now he had a godson to buy presents for. I saw him struggle to walk from the car to their house, but I saw no signs of pain when Michael got down on the floor to give Giovany his present. Little Giovany squealed and danced with joy when the fire engine's siren sounded, and Michael joined Giovany in his happy dance, all pain forgotten in the joy of the moment. His laughter brought tears to my eyes.

But I wonder what next development time will place on our doorstep. Michael's memory gets weaker almost by the day. He calls for me to come to his room, and by the time I arrive, he has forgotten why he called me. He tries to tell me about something he saw on the news, and he struggles to find the words. He tires more easily than ever, and waking from a nap leaves him confused as to the time, the day, and even the month. I feel that he is slipping away, and there's nothing I can do.

I can brush it aside if he snaps at me. And it doesn't bother me if he asks the same question 20 times a day, or if he wants to visit the game store, not remembering we went this morning. I only have a couple of medicines to protect his mental faculties from diminishing, but he resists taking them. Michael has entrusted everything he is and has to me; all I can do is try to keep him comfortable and maybe bring him a little happiness.

Time is so precious. I don't know how much time he has left. I have tried to contact some of those old friends to come and visit. He so appreciates a call, a card, or especially a visit. It seems everyone is too busy. But a visit now while he still knows them will mean more than a truckload of flowers at his funeral. I just wish they would give up a few hours of their time, their precious time, to bring a little bit of cheer to a dying man.

A Second Opinion

"**M**r. Brooks," Dr. Richards asked, "Can you tell me what day it is?" Michael looked back and forth from me to the doctor, hoping I would give him the answer. "Monday," he guessed.

"Are you sure?" she asked.

"Wednesday," he blurted out, just a bit too loud.

Surely the doctor would see his condition now that she was actually interviewing him. "No, Mr. Brooks. Today is Thursday. Can you tell me the date?"

Michael paused, not knowing how to respond. She repeated her question. "Seven nine fifty-eight" Michael said quickly. Puzzled, she asked again, and he gave the same quick answer

Dr. Richardson looked at me completely puzzled. "That's his birthdate," I explained.

She went one step further. "What season are we in, Mr. Brooks?" As hot as the weather had been I thought for sure he would know it was summer.

"It's winter," Michael answered. "I'll be glad when this cold weather is over."

At last she was starting to see the reasons for my worry, but it had been an uphill battle to bring her to this point. The two previous appointments she had completely disregarded my concerns.

"Doctor Richards," I pleaded, "Can you authorize longer in-home care? He only gets an hour a day. When I work, he is alone for at least 10 hours. If anything happened to him, he couldn't even call for help."

She hemmed and hawed, then reluctantly tossed me a bone. "Well, I suppose I COULD ask the social worker to make another assessment." I knew it could be a week before I heard anything, but at least I felt a little glimmer of hope.

I felt a little more encouraged when Ronnie, the social worker, called me the very next day. She had visited our home several times and knew Michael well. Once she knew his condition, she rushed to complete the assessment, delivering the form in person to Dr. Richards at 8:00 AM the following day.

Ronnie returned the following day to retrieve the form; it only needed three check marks and the doctor's signature. "It's on her desk," the receptionist told her - and closed the window in her face. Ronnie called daily, asking if the form was ready. 10 days passed and still she was told, "it's on her desk."

Frustrated and discouraged, the social worker was at an impasse. "I don't know what to do, Barry. I have no authority over Dr. Richards."

I drove 30 minutes to the office to give the receptionist my sincere appeal; but when I entered, I came face to face with open hostility. "Dr. Richards will complete your form when she is good and ready," she said with venom in her voice. "And don't be calling here harassing me."

Had I not witnessed it myself I would not have believed it. I had no qualms whatsoever about spending two hours on the phone wading through the maze of the Medicaid phone network to report what had occurred. With the roadblocks removed, we soon had a little more in-home care and a new physician.

I have brought Michael for his first examination in this new office. Dr. Werth treats Michael with the utmost respect, listening carefully to his comments. He may be 10 years younger than Michael or I; there is just a touch of gray in his hair. There's a smile on his face, and his eyes twinkle behind his glasses. The exam is gentle but thorough; he explains each step to Michael beforehand. Before long Michael tires and becomes confused; Dr. Werth directs the questions to me. He writes orders for blood work and a new ultrasound.

"What medications is Mr. Brooks taking?" he asks. I produce a long list and bag of prescription bottles. He examines the list in detail and his eyebrows go up. He names a certain medication and asks, "Why is he prescribed this?" I explain that the medication is for anxiety and that it helps prevent seizures.

Michael is completely tuned out, oblivious to our discussion. Nonetheless, Dr. Werth moves a little closer to me as he whispers. "Mr. Brooks' liver cannot filter that medication well. He MAY be experiencing a buildup in his bloodstream. You may wish to try reducing the amount. It could make a difference in his attention."

That same day I cut back on his anxiety medication. In a few days, Michael seemed a bit more alert. In a week, he was noticeably less confused. I was getting excited; he was coming back out of the dark.

About a month passed, and suddenly one morning Michael was BACK! He awoke sharp as a tack, hungry, feisty, and showing his old sense of humor. When I told him the date he was in shock; he had no memory of the previous four months.

I was amazed and thrilled to have my best friend back. I called Michael's mother and put him on the phone. They talked and laughed for an hour; he brought back events from years before with perfect clarity. I sat in the background, thrilled to see the old self again.

Dr. Werth has proved invaluable; he has helped me balance medications and understand Michael's condition better. The previous doctor had me believing that Michael was at death's door, and nothing could be done. But Dr. Werth examined and evaluated carefully before forming his opinions. He believes Michael has several good years left.

Michael still needs assistance and guidance; he has good days and some that are not good at all. But I am immeasurably thankful to have my best friend here a little longer.

CHAPTER 5

The Kitchen Sink

Sheila - A Portrait of Faithfulness

She stretches the phone cord to its limit and faces the wall as she talks. Sheila has a gravelly voice, difficult to understand over the phone, especially when she whispers privately to her husband. She raises her voice a bit in frustration - and then she tells him "don't cry" and "I'm sorry." She whispers "I'll see what I can do and call you later." Several times she says that she loves him.

I turn away, pretending I didn't hear any of the conversation, trying to preserve her dignity as best I can. I look at the prep sheet and ask her if we have enough shrimp for the day, trying to distract her and the others from personal matters.

In a few minutes she asks to speak to me privately. She needs to borrow some money again.

Sheila has been working here 14 years. Her hair is a salt and pepper mix - her face is heavily wrinkled. She wears magnifying glasses she bought at Walmart. Her teeth are in bad need of repair - a dentist would probably recommend a complete set of dentures - but where would she get the money?

Sheila tells me that her husband Tommy was in pain all night - the doctor treating him for cirrhosis of the liver prescribed a new medication yesterday. I loaned her money last week so their electricity wouldn't be turned off. Now she is asking for just six dollars to get a few items from the grocery store - just enough to last her until payday, when she will repay me part of her debt.

Tommy is trying to find work - but some days he is too ill. He calls every painter he knows, asking if they need an extra hand for the day. He wants to work, and does excellent work when someone will give him a chance.

Sheila asks for no handouts; she wants to pay her own way. But her wage just doesn't go far enough when Tommy isn't working.

At the restaurant she prepares coleslaw, tartar sauce, shrimp, cocktail sauce, and whatever new specials they introduce. Over the years she has prepared 145 tons of coleslaw, peeled, split and breaded 75 tons of shrimp, prepared 65,000 orders of onion rings, and dipped 4 million cups of tartar sauce. Day after day she prepares food, washes dishes, and sweeps and mops the same floor time and again. She has continued working as hundreds of others have come and gone. Sheila has stood by her husband through thick and thin; lately it has been mostly thin.

Last week Tommy was stronger. I paid him to paint my living room and hallway. He did excellent work, in short time, and cleaned up thoroughly behind himself. I got a difficult job done at a good price, and I think the work really did him some good. I hadn't seen Sheila smile so big in quite some time.

Things are tough; the company doesn't want to give her a raise and won't let her work long enough to earn overtime. But she doesn't complain. Sheila tries to do her best and earn every penny she can. She is looking for a second part-time job in the evenings. Tommy isn't able to work much, but she sticks by him, helping every way she can.

She is faithful to her husband. She is faithful to her employer. I don't see her getting any recognition for all she does. But I know Someone is watching over her and Tommy. God has weighed her in the balance, and found her faithful. He will be close to her, watch over her, and see that she and Tommy have what they need.

I hope when people look at my life that I will be considered as faithful as Sheila.

Karate Class

I had been on my feet since 10 a.m., and now past 9:00 p.m. I was glad we would be closing soon. My arm was itching and throbbing inside the heavy cast. For three weeks now I had been wearing this concrete torture device, ever since I fell roller skating with my daughter.

I was keeping an eye on three young men. I had seen them several times before. They were looking to stir up a little mischief. They might only succeed in annoying the cashier, or they might actually succeed in getting something for free. How I handled them tonight would determine if they would leave uninterested or if they would come back repeatedly, becoming a regular nuisance.

As one of the men asked my novice cashier various questions, the other two would interrupt and attempt to confuse her. I moved close behind her to bolster her and responded to the others, "She's waiting on your friend right now. She'll help YOU when he's finished."

The other two exchanged glances that said, "We ain't gonna get nothin' here," when one of them noticed my cast. "Hey man, you break your arm? Hey man, your arm broke?" I acted uninterested and helped fill the order as the others snickered.

"Hey, how'd you break your arm, man?" An idea popped into my head and instantly I knew how I would deal with these troublemakers.

"I broke it in karate class," I answered with a sigh as I stocked a display. All three of them burst into laughter. The ringleader stopped spluttering enough to ask more details.

"You broke it in karate class? What was you doing? How'd it happen?"

I had their undivided attention. They were nibbling at the bait.

I shrugged my shoulders and let out another sigh, as though bored with the whole ordeal. "We were having competitions. We had already completed two levels. It was my turn and I was going to break three concrete blocks. I was in mid-swing when someone sneezed. It broke my concentration, and this is what happened to me."

Two of the fellows were snickering, but they were too interested in the story to lose control. The ringleader stood right in front of me now, studying the cast and sizing me up as a karate student. "So, how bad did you get hurt? Will you still be able to do karate?"

The other two drew a little closer. They were all biting on the bait now. "Oh, I hit the blocks full force. I shattered the bone from the wrist to the elbow. It will be a good while before I can go back to karate class."

All three were right in front of me now, gazing at my arm, wondering how badly it hurt. The leader wanted to know more. "You shattered the bone? How long does that take to heal?"

I gave another sigh, as though I had told the story a number of times. They were just about to swallow the hook. "The surgery took several hours. They removed all the bone fragments and replaced it with a steel rod."

The three exchanged glances back and forth. "Hey man, will you be able to do karate with that arm?"

"Oh, yeah," I said with a gleam in my eye. "I can't wait till it heals. With a steel rod in this arm, I am really going to bust some heads, now."

All three started laughing, but the laughter quickly died away. The first one cast glances at his buddies and then backed away. He walked to the door without another word. The other two snickered a moment and then they too drew silent. Discovering their leader gone, they left too, looking over their shoulders as they exited.

Once they were gone, my crew fell to the floor laughing. They had kept silent, knowing my tale was pure hogwash, but as mesmerized as the visitors at my fabrication. We never saw the annoying trio again.

The Bird Nest Symposium

Several millennia ago, birds enjoyed an organized society; globally fowl of all kind communicated with one another and exchanged ideas.

One day the owls were discussing the less fortunate (and less intelligent) birds and concluded they could offer assistance through their well-recognized intelligence. The owls voted and, believing this was a wonderful idea, invited bird ambassadors from every continent to come and attend the First International Bird Nest Symposium.

Had you or I been there we would have been surprised at the variety and the orderliness of the emissaries. There were large birds such as eagles and osprey, and small ones such as titmice and hummingbirds. There were plainly dressed wrens and sparrows, and there were colorful ones ranging from parrots to grandiose peacocks. Some were quiet and modest, but loud and chattering varieties were present as well.

The crowd settled in, and the owls asked the group to listen as their moderator took the stump to address the crowd. "Fine feathered friends," were his first words, and immediately the penguins raised an objection, having no feathers. The speaker apologized, and began again. "Dear birds of many nations, it has come to our attention that there are many poor species in our numbers who are suffering. We have called you together in order that we may take pity on the less fortunate. Many of our species do not have the know-how to create appropriate housing.

"We organized this Bird Nest Symposium to determine the best method for making a nest, and to carry those instructions back to all our bird countries and assist those needy birds."

All agreed this was an excellent idea, but no matter what the speaker suggested, various members objected. When the owls suggested nests should be placed in a hollow in a tree trunk, many birds argued to the contrary. The eagles said nests must be high to see a great distance; the whip-poor-wills said nests must be on the ground for concealment. Robins said the best placement was on an open branch where they could see predators approaching. They could reach no agreement on where the proper nest should be built.

So the owls redirected the discussion to the proper material for nest building. Ospreys stated the nest should be built of large sticks and branches. The hummingbirds stated that the best materials were moss, lichens, and spider silk. Crows and magpies said it didn't matter so long as you included something shiny or sparkling. The ostrich said that a huge pile of decaying vegetation protected their eggs well and kept them warm, too.

Swallows swore that mud was the best material, and nothing could change their mind. The weaverbirds declared that the only safe nest was one woven of long grasses, suspended from a branch where it could swing in the wind. The penguins, sandpipers, and terns were in a camp of their own, failing to understand all the arguing about building materials. The penguins stated that just a circle of stones made an excellent nest, while the sandpipers and terns contended that a depression in the sand suited them perfectly. The wrens and bluebirds felt that a sheltered area was best for a nest, no matter whether it was in a tree or under the eaves of a cliff.

The speaker owl looked at the dodos, who weren't saying anything. "What do you think we should make our nests from?" the moderator asked them.

"Nests? Nests?" the dodos said, looking at one another. "What are nests?"

At the back of the crowd, the cowbird and the cuckoo were huddled together, whispering. "I don't care what they say is the best nest," the cowbird told the cuckoo. "I am still going to let some other bird do the work, and I will just lay my eggs in his nest."

Before long, the group became louder and louder, each convinced that its own nesting method was the best and tred to show its merits to the other species.

The buzzards and vultures began to complain "When are you going to serve refreshments? You didn't expect us to come all this way and not be fed, did you?"

The eagle flapped and shouted, "Enough of this nonsense! I don't need anyone telling me how to make my nest. I'm leaving." The stork and the hawk agreed and took to the sky. The penguins began waddling toward the water, followed by pelicans and geese.

The owls called out, begging the birds to stay. "There is so much more to discuss. We need to decide who can contribute nesting materials for the less fortunate."

Therefore, the symposium dissolved, having accomplished nothing. But even today, there are owls in our midst - I imagine you may have met a few. If you are different, they look down upon you as uneducated or less fortunate. They have appointed themselves as judge and jury, and they want to instruct you the correct way to dress, to talk, to work, to worship, or to raise a family, or even what constitutes a family.

I don't claim to know it all, and I certainly don't possess any secret knowledge, but in my few years, I have learned some questions don't have a single correct answer. It doesn't matter if you live in a shack or a mansion, in an apartment or a tent. But if you care for those around you, if you are honest, if you can give and forgive, if you can love, there is a great deal right in your life.

Profile of Courage: Martha

Faith in God has many manifestations, many evidences in the lives of its possessors. Courage is a fruit of faith; this is a profile of the courage that I see in Martha.

Martha is a 40 year old Christian woman from Ecuador living in the United States on a work visa. She came to the US three and a half years ago to help support her family, who wait for her in Ecuador. Jobs are more difficult to find there and don't offer the pay available here.

Martha's English isn't very good, and she speaks with a thick accent. But it doesn't stop her from working and from communicating. Martha has held several different jobs in the past few years, usually two at the same time. For a while she worked at two different restaurants; when employees at one mistreated her, she left that job for another. She worked a short time at a clothing warehouse, but long hours and heavy lifting were too demanding.

Martha now works five days a week at one restaurant and at a Hispanic salon on weekends; she likes both jobs, but she especially enjoys working at the salon. The she can interact freely in her own language and performs the same work she did in Ecuador.

She has also moved several times, renting a room from a family or sharing an apartment with other Latinos. Like many people coming to the US for work, she doesn't mind small living spaces. Comforts and conveniences are not her reasons for working in the US; her only reason for being here is to help her family.

In Ecuador, waiting for her return, are three teenage daughters and a husband. Her husband was not granted a visa; he works as a teacher earning in an entire month what Martha earns in one week at the restaurant. Martha buys calling cards to talk with her family twice a week. Even with rent, utilities, and grocery expenses, she earns enough to send money and clothing home to her husband and girls; clothing is far less expensive here than in her home country.

One night as we closed up the restaurant, Martha asked me about the small white flakes falling from the sky. When I explained that it was snow, she was fascinated. She had never seen snow except in pictures and thought it fell in one fell swoop as a blanket. The following day I took a photo of her standing in the snow for her to mail home to Ecuador.

If you ask about her family, she always has photos and will gladly tell you about her three girls. And when you ask her how long it has been since she has seen them, she will probably wipe a tear or two from her eyes.

In Ecuador Martha regularly attended a Catholic church with her family. Although there are Spanish speaking churches in Charlotte, Martha has not connected with any of them. She works seven days a week and knows no one at those churches. Each night she lies down tired from her labors, but glad that she has the ability to work and send money back home. Holidays are difficult for her as they stir up memories and longings her family.

Martha misses her family and her country a great deal, but she doesn't mind her sacrifice. You will not hear her complain. Faith and love brought her here to support her family; when she feels that it is no longer necessary, she will gladly return to Ecuador.

James 2:18 Yea, a man may say, Thou hast faith, and I have works: show me thy faith without thy works, and I will show thee my faith by my works.

Courage is not the absence of fear; courage faces danger and difficulty and struggles through them. Martha has courage. Her courage comes from her faith in God and her love for her family. We could learn a lot from her.

What's in YOUR Medicine Chest?

Every home has a medicine chest, and most contain a variety of potions for common ailments. Yours probably contains

Tylenol, some Lomotil, some Kaopectate, and maybe even a cough syrup as potent as Vicks 44 or an ointment tried and true like Mentholatum.

But as good as those remedies may be, they are NOT enough; they only treat a few simple symptoms.

If I have a bad cold or the flu, I need more than just a few pills. Some Nyquil may help, but it's the extra treatments that truly promote healing. I have a special quilt and a heating pad that I pull out of the closet, reserved for times of achiness and shivering. Those items bring some comfort, but Mama's pitcher, filled with her hot lemonade, induces the medicine to work and puts me on the mend.

What kind of medicine do you take when you are feeling the effects of your years? Arthritis Pain Formula may ease the joints somewhat, but I know a tonic that will help you feel better much faster. A few special photos of your sweetheart, back when you were both younger and more attractive will perk up your circulation and put some color in your cheeks, a lot better than that Excedrin will. A snuggle up on the sofa with your loved one will put that spring back in your step.

Are you feeling depressed? Do you feel discouraged over a lack of accomplishment? Anytime I suffer from that complaint, I call my son or my daughter. I hear their cheerful voices describe accomplishments at work, and I think of the years I spent raising them. I look upon them and I see my life's greatest work. Any feelings of inadequacy or purposelessness vanish like a puff of smoke.

Or maybe you just have a case of the blahs. Everyone gets that once in a while; my prescription for that ailment is a short drive to the nearest Baskin-Robbins. I don't know what your chemistry requires, but a double dip of pistachio in a waffle cone always clears it up for me. A harmless indulgence and a break from routine gives me the stamina to return to the normal grind of day-to-day work.

Maybe the most peculiar item in my medicine chest is a well-used VHS tape. It is reserved for a really pitiful ailment I get maybe once a year, usually following a really, really rotten day at work. It is the day when everyone calls in sick, there is twice as much work to do, and nothing goes right. I screw up orders, I misplace important phone numbers, I forget a customer's name, and I have to work extra hours in addition to everything else.

My tape is an old Jerry Lewis movie, *Who's Minding the Store?* It probably wouldn't do anything for you, but the silly antics, the bumbling, and the gold paint poured on top of Ray Walston's head make me laugh out loud. I forget my trivial grumbles. My favorite segment is the skit of Jerry Lewis pecking away ridiculously on an invisible typewriter. It's a silly prescription I know, but it works.

You might want to consider restocking your medicine chest with some different elixirs and tonics than you have been using. Maybe in addition to the Tylenol and Motrin, you need to put the phone number of an old friend in one of those medicine bottles or maybe a CD of some special music to cheer you up when you are feeling down. There is a lot more to medicine and feeling better than just taking a pill.

A Different Kind of Thanks

Whenever holidays come around, I get nostalgic, and Thanksgiving is no different. I could reminisce about Mama's delicious specialties and the gathering of relatives at Grandma's, but I thought I should share something recent to express thankfulness. It isn't that dramatic, but I do feel it speaks of God's protection and provision.

I have watched many people use cellular phones and often said, "I'm glad I don't have a job that demands I use one." It seemed they were busy and frantic, lacking time to eat a meal uninterrupted. And I had personally witnessed examples of drivers who became dangerous by preoccupation with the phone they held.

But when I thought about how much time I am on the road, and I saw a great offer, something nudged me to buy it. After a week, I still barely knew how to use it, confusing the address book and misfiling numbers repeatedly. I was wondering if my purchase had been a hasty mistake.

And then my car broke down on I-85, 10 miles outside of Charlotte.

I called AAA and arranged towing to a garage near my home. Then I called work and told them I was having car trouble and would be late. Then I called a friend to ask if he could come and pick me up at the garage and lend me his car for a day. The little handheld phone had saved me a world of trouble.

But I wasn't thankful so much for a phone. I was much more thankful for the understanding this brief incident revealed. I have broken down on the road before, and believe me, it was no picnic. I was thankful I didn't have to walk a mile or more to a phone. I was thankful I didn't have to struggle to find change to make those calls. I was thankful I know an honest mechanic to repair my car. I was thankful that I had a job to call and tell I would be late, and that I wouldn't be discharged for it. And I was thankful to have a friend kind enough to meet me at the garage and loan me his car.

It only took a minor incident to change my point of view about cell phones. And it only took a few moments for me to see reasons for thankfulness.

Pardon me a moment while I step up behind the pulpit. Too often we tend to think "what have I got to be thankful for?" Or we consider thankfulness so high and lofty that we practice it only for a short time, once a year. Thankfulness should be an attitude, a way of life, a manner of walk and talk. With just a wee bit of effort, you can see your life from a different point of view. Perhaps you will recognize that maybe you, too, have daily examples of Someone watching over you.

The Perfect Stocking

Over the years Christmas has never lost its magic for me; even before Thanksgiving I am thinking about putting up the tree and making Christmas goodies. I try to make Christmas not just an exchanging of gifts, but a childish romp that lasts all month.

One of the things I enjoy most is filling the Christmas stockings. Even though my kids are now adults, they still enjoy their stockings; I heartily recommend that everyone in the family receive a stocking. In my home even the two dogs and two cats get a miniature stocking filled with tasty treats.

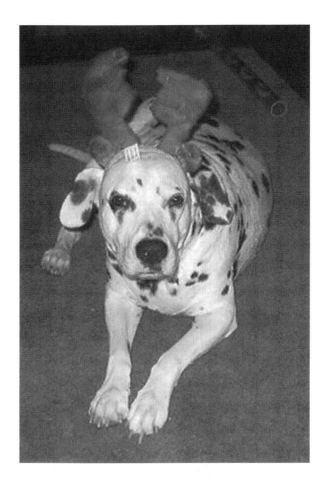

It has come to my attention that some of you do not enjoy Christmas, and a few even dread it; this is an atrocity. The only reason I can imagine for this reaction is that someone stopped giving you a properly filled Christmas stocking some years ago. Therefore I have undertaken to give a few instructions on preparing the perfect Christmas stocking.

First, the preferred color is fire engine red; other colors are acceptable, but a thick, velvety material is necessary. If you have ever given one of those red net, pre-packed dime-store stockings, you are banished to sit in the corner for 15 minutes and think about the errors of your ways.

Second, the object of filling the stocking is fun; it should be fun to empty it, and it should be fun to watch others discover its contents. Silly items are fine and a certain percentage of the stocking SHOULD be silly. Pez candies and dispensers fit this category, as do yo-yo's and Bolo paddles.

Sweets are an absolute necessity; the stocking should be tailored to the particular tastes of the recipient. Chocolate covered cherries, Hershey's kisses, books of LifeSavers, bubble gum, and taffy are all fine ingredients. Bottles of bubbles have been a fun item in our stockings for many years. We are also fond of Barnum's animal crackers. An item which shows up every other year or so is the famous nose and eyebrow glasses. A photo of everyone in the family wearing those silly glasses will likely be a priceless treasured one.

When the recipient is not a young child, something of a little bit of value is greatly appreciated in the stocking. For teenage girls, CD's, fingernail polish of various colors, and small pieces of jewelry are thrilling additions. For the teenage boys, it may be a little harder. Comic books, a new cartridge to the video game system, or a new CD may be in order. If they are legal in your state, fireworks always please boys (of ANY age.)

For a spouse, the stocking requires more thought and planning. Sweets, silly, and practical all need to combine for a successful stocking. For the wife, a bit of the favorite candies, a cutesy figurine declaring your love, and a silly trinket all bring smiles and add surprise when in the TOE of the stocking is a special piece of jewelry. A necklace, a pair of earrings, or a brooch will have special sentimental value if it is the last item in a stocking full of fun items.

For the husband, sweets, peanuts, snack items (maybe a pack of expensive cigars for the tobacco fancier) can cover up a new tool for the toolbox buried far beneath towards the toe. But don't be fooled; behind that rough exterior, he gets a kick out of Pez candy dispensers, bubble gum, and a little flashlight, too. Just go in the other room and peek around the corner; he will probably be playing with the flashlight and the bubbles.

Each family will find one or more items that get an especially good reaction and will become yearly traditions. Over the years two items have become essential for the successful Christmas stockings in my family. First, there MUST be a box of Cracker Jack, preferably towards the toe so it has to be sought after. But the absolute crowning glory and *piece de resistance* is a can of Silly String; everyone must have a can, sitting right on top of the stocking, for a silly string fight first thing on Christmas morning. Once the string has been shot and all have been chased around the living room, you can settle down for the fun of watching everyone empty the stockings and enjoy the silliness.

I hope all of you have paid close attention and will be following these directives in the preparation of your stockings this year. I will be dropping by, and anyone who gets an F for a grade will have to wash the dishes from Christmas dinner for your entire neighborhood. So, get out there, fill those stockings and have fun!

Where DO Grits Come From?

In college several classmates and I often shared breakfast together. On this particular morning five of us were enjoying a typical breakfast of bacon and scrambled eggs, biscuits, coffee, and the most important ingredient, GRITS.

We chatted about research papers and tests, and as we enjoyed our meal, Melvin, a student from New York stopped at our table. "Mind if I join you?" he asked politely.

We mumbled agreement and carried on as before. Trying to strike up a conversation, he looked at his plate and said, "I've always wondered, where do grits come from?"

I paused just a second and said, "They grow on trees."

Melvin looked at his plate, wondering how that white steaming mound of grits had come to him from a tree. The others at the table gave me a puzzled look and I winked, saying nothing. They caught on to my joke and waited to see how the situation would develop.

After a momentary pause, he started to nibble. "I never heard of grit trees before."

Without looking up, I replied, "It's too cold up North. They won't grow there."

The others around the table listened attentively, now really curious to see how this tale would unravel. Melvin went a little further and asked, "What do they look like?"

Here I added some details, some icing on the cake. "Well, they look a lot like a Bradford pear tree but not as tall. The leaves are dark green on top and silver on the back. And the whole tree turns a brilliant yellow in the fall."

All my friends were interested now, eager to participate in the ruse. When the next question came, Ann jumped in. Melvin asked what the fruit looked like and she responded. "They're about the size of a cantaloupe. First they are green, then yellow, and when they turn white, they're ripe."

Mike joined in, too. "We have a grit tree in our backyard, and my Mom always picks them yellow and lets them ripen on the windowsill."

Melvin accepted all this in as perfectly genuine. We were all so knowledgeable and helpful. "Okay, then, how do you get from this big white thing the size of a cantaloupe to this white stuff?"

It was my turn again. "That's easy. You just take the grit, put it in the top of your grit grinder, turn the handle a few times and voilà! You have a bowl of grits."

Lynn spoke up at this point. "Does your Mom still use one of those? I thought everybody had an electric grit grinder by now."

The conversation died down for a minute, and Melvin seemed satisfied. Then he asked another question, "So grits are a big business in the South, huh?"

Ann picked up the ball again. "It sure is. Buren over there is from Talladega, and his family has grit tree orchards."

Everyone looked at Buren, the quietest and meekest of our little clan. If anyone would blow the game, I felt it would be him. "Well," Buren drawled, blushing at the sudden attention, "of course, it used to be a grit plantation back in the old days." It was all I could do to keep from bursting out laughing.

Melvin was quite impressed. He had no idea grits were so common and so plentiful. He sat up a little taller and ate his grits with more respect.

And then I went too far. "I know a family in town who is so rich, they have hot and cold running grits in their kitchen."

Melvin froze, his fork halfway from the plate to his mouth. He sat immobile as his eyes x-rayed every person around the table, recalling every comment. Abruptly he flung his napkin into the plate, stood up, and carried his tray to another table.

Strangest thing, he never sat with us for breakfast again. Come to think of it, he never even spoke to any of us anymore. I wonder if he thinks of us when he hears the word "grits."

Did You Hear That?

I hope I am not alone and others are hearing these voices. When I was little Mama taught me listening to that "still small voice" would keep me out of trouble. But now I am hearing a lot of little voices, and I'm not sure they have my best interests in mind.

It started last week at Waldenbooks. "Pssst, psst" I heard. I looked all around, not seeing anyone.

There it was again, "Psst! Hey you, over here!" I looked over in the next aisle. It was coming from a cookbook on the shelf. "Up here, up here. Take me down and look at this chocolate cake on my cover. The recipe is on page 427. It's easy, and I can tell by looking at you that you like sweets."

I had to admit that cake looked scrumptious, but that comment about my liking sweets got my attention. I already have a number of cookbooks, mostly for desserts. I put the book down and walked away.

Around the corner a display of children's books caught my eye, and I flipped through one. The book sighed in my hand, "Don't you know a nice little boy who wants a picture book? My pretty pictures can help him learn to read." It was a gorgeous book, and I was sorry that I didn't know a child to give it to. The book moaned in disappointment when I put it back on the shelf.

Around the corner there were a number of different voices, but they weren't talking to me. "Oh, I hope he doesn't buy me; I'll sit on the shelf and he'll never pick me up again. Don't worry. He won't buy any of us. He doesn't know a thing about computers." As I turned away, I heard a sigh of relief and several chuckles.

Those books knew too much about me. I decided not to buy any books that day and left hurriedly.

I didn't hear any more voices for a few days. But when I went grocery shopping, it started all over again. I was looking for some potatoes and carrots to cook a pot roast when that familiar "psst, psst" arose from the produce section.

A cabbage was calling to me. "Hey, mister! Put me in your buggy. I've got connections at the meat counter. I'll get you a deal on the best corned beef brisket in the store." It sounded like a good idea to me.

Then the pasta aisle had a long conversation with me. In the end I decided to take home several different pastas and sauces and try them all in turn.

On the beverage aisle, the wines and liquors didn't have too much to say to me. They saw I had made friends with a six-pack of Miller, and nothing they had to say would change my mind. I think I heard a sauvignon blanc and a cabernet whispering something about a hillbilly and a redneck, but I didn't really care to hear their opinions, so I left.

I tried to avoid the cookies and desserts. Honest, I did! But my buggy insisted that was the shortest way to the checkout. Every sweet and confection was talking to me, tempting me. I threw two packages in the buggy and ran for the checkout before I was overwhelmed.

But even at the checkout, the battle wasn't over. All the candy bars were talking to me, and all the tabloids were staring at me, but I ignored them all. I paid the cashier and strolled out to my car.

I thought I would be safe once I started home, but there was a terrible clamor from the back seat. The groceries were arguing among themselves as to which was going to be cooked tonight. Not one of them would take "no" for an answer.

So I am inviting you to come on over for supper. It seems I have enough to feed a crowd, and it's all ready and waiting right now. I have corned beef and cabbage, pot roast, mashed potatoes, spaghetti and meatballs, lasagna, meatloaf, cookies, pineapple upside-down cake, banana pudding, fried chicken, rice and gravy, green beans, mushroom-rice casserole, and a few more things still in the oven, the microwave, and the crockpot.

Please hurry and come on over before I cook anything else. And maybe you could stop at the drugstore on the way and pick me up a set of earplugs. I really need to stop these voices so I can get some rest.

Thank you, Miss Frances

Miss Frances was a short thin woman, certainly no taller than 5 feet. She had never married, and she was near 60 years old when I studied 11th grade English in her class. Her thin hair was straight and mostly gray. She wore ordinary plaid dresses that hung loosely on her delicate frame. On her feet were flat bottom shoes and bobbie socks. Her voice was soft and delicate. I never heard it raised louder than a conversational volume. It would have taken a great imagination to call her attractive.

But there was something about this gentle spinster that defied explanation. Regardless of the noise and commotion in the hallway, her classroom was always quiet and orderly. No matter what horrible events occurred in the news, there was a studious atmosphere in Miss Frances' room.

Miss Frances did not permit idle chatter or interruptions of her instruction; if someone whispered or tried to pass a note, she stopped it in an instant. She simply looked up from her book, called the student's name, and paused. Immediately the talking ceased, the notes were put away, and English became the center of attention again.

Miss Frances shared her gentle dignity with every student she taught and every person she met. I was stumped how there could be so many students who had never diagrammed a sentence, did not know the difference between subject and verb, and had never heard of the classic authors. But Miss Frances never batted an eye, no matter how poorly the student was prepared. She accepted everyone regardless of color, background, and ability and encouraged all to learn. She never made anyone feel inferior in any way.

I saw big hulking football players who towered over Miss Frances and could have broken her tiny frame like a twig. But in this classroom, they were quiet, meek, and did their best to comprehend Shakespeare and to recite poems by Browning and Wordsworth. Yet in other classes, loud threatening coaches couldn't get even minimal effort from the same students. To this day I wonder what secret she possessed.

Miss Frances had a plan for each day's lessons, and she would not let distractions prevent her from teaching. One day water began leaking heavily through the ceiling, right where Miss Frances was accustomed to stand and lecture. Apparently something had occurred in the chemistry lab directly above our class, but a little bit of water was not going to prevent

Miss Frances from reading *The Canterbury Tales.* She dispatched one student to report the leak and to be certain it was nothing volatile while she continued her lesson. I will never forget the image of tiny Miss Frances, reading Chaucer as a muscle-bound athlete stood and held an umbrella over her.

I moved away from Clinton in 1985, but during visits home I often dropped in to visit Miss Frances. We would sit on her screened porch as she read my latest article or story. She gently pointed out errors or inconsistencies, encouraging me to find my own mistakes and correct them. But at the same time, she took great pride in every word, as though she were a proud parent, not a teacher.

Miss Frances, I was sorry to hear that you passed away last year. I have vague memories of a few instructors from all my education, but you were more than just a teacher. You gave me dignity; the greatest thing you taught me was not how to write an essay or a critical analysis. More than anything else, you taught me to believe in myself.

I miss you, Miss Frances. Thank you for being my friend.

God DOES have a Sense of Humor

There are times when I get so wrapped up in my own self-importance that I lose sight of the truly important. At those points I could use a good kick in the pants to wake me up and show me how foolish I have become. This little tale describes one of those wake up calls.

A few years ago there was an upsurge within Christian teaching now referred to as "the Prosperity Movement." It doesn't matter who started the ball rolling. It began as a series of sermons teaching how God wanted His people to pray and ask for what they needed. But somehow, the teaching went a little out of bounds. Using verses pulled out of context and stories that may have stretched the truth, teachers began telling believers to pray for new jobs, new houses, and cars.

But they didn't stop there. They went on urging their listeners to pray for anything and everything, whether it was practical and needed or not. "If you want it, ask for it. God wants you to PROSPER." They used verses to demonstrate how to corner God into answering your every request.

The teachings grew like snowballs, getting bigger with each sermon and each new testimony more fantastic than the last. Now I believe in prayer; I don't wish to demean it even a little bit. But things had gotten out of hand and God was being depicted as a giant genie, just waiting to fulfill our every whim, whether it was good for us or not.

For the most part, I saw this teaching as I describe it now. I liked hearing people uplift the power of prayer and praising God as able to fulfill any need. But somewhere, I got a little off center as well.

I had been listening to one of those television preachers, and I became rather full of myself. I remember one morning as I left for work I very boldly told God, "I want $50 in my hand before 5 o'clock this afternoon." I pointed to my left hand and arrogantly nodded my head, confident that I would get $50. It didn't matter that there was money in my billfold and in the bank. I just wanted to prove that I could ask and it would happen.

I drove 45 minutes to work and numerous events during the day distracted me so that I forgot my ostentatious demand. That afternoon I traveled across town to purchase parts to repair a broken piece of equipment. On the return trip I had a flat tire and discovered my spare was useless. Eventually I ended up at Firestone to buy some new tires.

I walked across the street to use the ATM, getting some cash to supplement what was already in my wallet.

As I took the money from the slot I heard a voice say, "Look at your hand." I looked down at the receipt and the cash. The voice spoke again, "There's your $50."

I had to laugh. I fully deserved that comeuppance and more. "Thank you," I told God as I chuckled, slapping my forehead with the other hand. "I deserved that."

As I drove home that day, I talked with Him further, laughing at His sense of humor and at my own foolishness. I still pray just as much, but I realize that I am only a petitioner, not the master.

Food of the Gods

Last night on the History Channel I enjoyed a program on ancient Greek and Roman mythology. Years ago I read *The Odyssey*, and I always considered those tales just childish entertainment. The myths of Circe, the Sirens, Pegasus, the Cyclops, and more were just nighttime stories for youngsters.

But the speaker referred to a myth which disturbed me because I fear others might actually believe this tale. In horror, I am undertaking to correct this fallacy lest the world be further misled.

In mythology, Mount Olympus of Greece is hailed as the home of the gods. Without going into a long religious debate, I will state that I know the genuine location of that magical mountain. The true mountain is in the area of Landrum, South Carolina, and can be seen from miles away while traveling north on I-26 from Spartanburg to Asheville. And the Elysian Fields, a paradise reserved for the blessed, are nowhere near Greece or Rome. Their true site is a small plot of farmland pasture, down a weary country road near Campobello, South Carolina. In this secret plot, bordered on one side by a peach orchard and on the other by a barnyard surrounded by huge black walnut trees, there is a magic which makes it paradisiacal. The lower end of the pasture leads into a forest where flows a cold trickling stream, filled with glittering pebbles and surrounded by wild ferns. As a child I often played in this pasture and drank from the cold stream as I searched it for gold and for arrowheads.

The myth which disturbed me most was that the gods of Mount Olympus consumed AMBROSIA which gave them their immortality. Reportedly the gods gave this divine food to man.

Now, I have eaten ambrosia. This mixture of pineapple, banana and coconut might be tasty, and I suppose it may contain enough vitamin C to ward off a cold. But I certainly wouldn't call it the food of the gods, and it won't make any human immortal.

I will reveal a family secret, a food which DOES have miraculous properties. This food has been passed down over the centuries, and in my lifetime from my grandmother, to my mother, to me and to my children. The secret food is RICE and GRAVY.

My grandfather once told me that the original recipe was given to Methuselah by an angel, but after 900 years the Biblical saint decided that man shouldn't live that long and altered the recipe. There are tales and family folklore about miraculous events across the span of history, but I will only refer to a few of the most recent events.

During the Civil War there was a troop of Confederate soldiers who were undefeated during most of their campaign. No matter how severe their injuries, they would drag themselves back to camp, where after a meal, they were cured and would return to battle with the same vigor and strength as before. One of my ancestors was the cook for this troop; he fed them rice and gravy. Upon learning of this secret, Union soldiers captured my relative and held him behind Union lines. Without rice and gravy that company became just like all the other troops and soon perished. Had my ancestor continued cooking for the Confederate troops, the outcome of the war might have been different.

During the 1890's, a famous speaker was passing through South Carolina when he suffered a heart attack. The attending physician advised him to make preparations for the hereafter as he had only a matter of minutes to live; my great-grandfather fed the dying man a few spoons of rice and gravy. In minutes he was on his horse, continuing on his journey. Word of his imminent death had already escaped, however, and at his next engagement the speaker made the famous comment, "Reports of my death have been highly exaggerated." He never revealed that rice and gravy had cured him.

Two years ago, following cancer surgery, I was on morphine several days for pain. I tried to explain to my surgeon what I needed to recover, but he gave strict orders to keep me on a liquid diet. Finally released from the hospital, the first thing I did was to cook a generous amount of rice and gravy. After the first bite, my pain left me and my strength began to return.

And just last week in downtown Charlotte, a man fell 9 stories from a construction site. He suffered a punctured lung, a skull fracture, and 14 broken bones. While ambulance workers radioed for a medivac helicopter, I pulled a cup of rice and gravy from my lunchbox and gave the man a bite. Immediately his lung was restored. I gave him another bite, and his skull was whole again. At this point he sat up and took the cup from me. In a few minutes he was walking around, saying he was ready to get back to work.

There are many more tales across the years of how rice and gravy has brought people back from the brink of death, so now I am sending samples to the Mayo Clinic, the CDC in Atlanta, the White House and the Pentagon. I am willing to share this family secret so the miraculous qualities of this heavenly food can be fully researched.

If you ever visit me for a meal, you can rest assured that among the other items on the table will be enough rice and gravy for everyone to have two helpings or more. Mythology may have gotten the details a bit confused. Although this supernatural food may not make man immortal, it comes pretty darn close.

P.S. A cartoonist once created a comic strip based on the exploits of my family, changing names to protect our identities. L'il Abner's true last name was actually Holcomb, and it was Holcomb-berry tonic that enabled Mammy to see visions and gave L'il Abner his phenomenal strength.

But that's ANOTHER story.

CHAPTER 6

Time Draws Short

The Passage of Time, the Passage of Me

A nd now I see I am entering a new chapter of my life. Finalizing this manuscript has brought back many memories - some wonderful, and some difficult to swallow. But they are just memories. Time goes on whether we choose to allow it or not.

1999 was a year of transition for me. My marriage was over. My kids would be on their own in just a few years. I downsized to a smaller house, and of all things, I bought a cute little sports car. This was quite a change after driving station wagons and family vehicles for 20 years. The same year I acquired my first pager; I commuted so much I felt my daughter should be able to contact me at any time. I bought my first real computer; not like the Apple II-E I wore out with the constant changing of floppy discs, but a real computer with a printer, scanner, and internet access. I thought I was really something.

When I pointed these things out to my daughter, her response did not flatter me. "Well, Dad," Adria pointed out. "It's about time." I soon realized it had taken me until the last year of the millennium to arrive in the 90's.

Still, I dragged my feet, longing for the past. I filled my home with memorabilia and autographs of celebrities long gone and nearly forgotten. I still had a TV antenna on my roof when everyone else was watching cable. While walking the dogs I noticed my house sported the only antenna for many surrounding blocks.

My kids laughed when I complained about having to pay to pump air into my tires. I finally accepted that it was no longer free, but I still thought of pedaling my bicycle to Chick's Grocery where I could pump up all the bicycle tires, inner tubes, and floats I wanted for nothing. But when I stopped for air at a convenience store by South Park, I was infuriated. Not only did they charge 75 cents for a few squirts of air, they had the audacity to refuse cash. The only method of payment accepted by this rinky-dink machine was a CREDIT CARD! I was insulted.

Gradually, a page has turned and a realization has come. I have met others my own age who are wonderful people of faith, and THEY are not stuck in the past. They work in varied occupations, and while I would not consider them worldly, they are well-informed and up-to-date with the latest technology. I began to see that holding onto my Firestone LP's of Doris Day and Robert Goulet singing Christmas carols and my VHS tape collection of Victor Borge wasn't really helping me.

Just yesterday I realized one of my tires was a bit low. As I drove to the convenience store, I remembered some of my previous articles. The first piece I sold was a sci-fi story about a teenager who traveled into the past to witness events he believed in. I was 17 when I wrote it. And the very first article I wrote for The Clinton Chronicle was entitled "Turn Back the Clock." In that essay I reminisced of store fronts and people I remembered when I was 6 or 7 years old. Maybe, I surmised, it IS time to let things go.

Actually, I may have stumbled onto the memory of when my fascination with time and the past began. I was standing in my Great Aunt Trudy's parlor; it was filled with musty old sofas with doilies on the arms and marble-topped end tables. On the mantle was a beautiful clock with a spinning pendulum. I stood there transfixed, watching the golden spheres beneath the glass dome spin one way and then the other. Was that when I became mesmerized and stuck in a bygone era? Ever after and still today I am fascinated by tales of time travel.

Pondering a little more seriously, I think of the wonderful people in my church. God hasn't changed. He is still just as loving and forgiving as He was in the past. Maybe it's not that there were more people of integrity and faith in previous decades; maybe it's just that we see so much negativity in the media, and people of honesty and sacrifice don't attract the camera's speedily changing focus. There are no fewer people who live for God now; they just aren't concerned about others knowing it.

I still love to tell the stories of the "good ol' days" when I could go to the Broadway theater with a dollar, buy all the popcorn, candy, and soda pop I could consume in two hours and still come out with change. But I really must admit, it took a lot longer to earn a dollar back then. Yes, Mama could feed our family of four for two weeks on $20, but it took both my parents working to have that much available for groceries.

At this very moment my house is in complete turmoil. I have decided to renovate my kitchen, replacing the linoleum, countertops, range, oven, light fixtures, cabinets and even wiring that are original to when the house was built in 1960. The new kitchen will be slick, clean and up-to-date. My Gosh! I am still so far behind. It has taken me till 2011 to finally arrive in the 21st century.

I pull up to the air dispenser and read the instructions. It will cost me a dollar for one minute of air. I sift through my change and check. The machine requires quarters only or a credit card. I only have 3. I chuckled at myself and inserted a credit card. I better go ahead and accept it. I don't want to be left behind.

Epilogue

And so we arrive at the final page. The story does not end; it continues each day as events unfold and lives progress. This little volume contains only bits and pieces, highlights of one life and its intersections with others. Some stories have deliberately been omitted, because they were too dark, too bitter, or perhaps still incomplete or misunderstood. Others were passed over as too light or sarcastic. Perhaps there will be an additional volume or a revised version which will fill in some of the cracks and answer unspoken questions.

If what I have shared seems unbelievable, please consider this. My life has been filled with long periods of dull drudgery occasionally punctuated by moments of the Divine. The criteria which separates a miracle from the ordinary is the fact that is outside the realm of normal experience. THIS is what makes the occurrence extra-ordinary. These events happened over the span of a lifetime, not within a matter of weeks. Prayers uttered years ago are still shaping events and yielding fruit only now close to ripening.

In the walk of faith we experience seasons of wandering the desert and brief respites at oases from which we can glimpse the promised land. I usually experience a slow simmer of the Lord moving in my life, and occasionally I enjoy periods of a full rolling boil. At times I have knelt and wept. More than once sudden understandings have dawned on me, prompting me to jump up and shout as I burst into dance. But these are the extremes; 99.5% of my prayer life is quiet, methodical, and ordinary.

Sometimes I force myself to look at my life through glasses of reason. I grow very analytical, questioning and doubting every experience and every interpretation to which I have come. Can anyone verify this? Is that how it REALLY happened or only how I IMAGINE it happened? Was that real or am I lying to myself? I look at my life and wonder what I am becoming. Am I evolving into a mystic? Am I slipping off the deep end? In the end I always arrive at the same conclusion that right or wrong, I am still seeking God. I could stop breathing easier than I could stop this journey.

The fabric of my life is filled with silver and gold threads which transverse decades; there are also dark threads which do the same. (My friends will tell you I am often verbose. Please overlook all the mixed metaphors I have thrown at you.) As mentioned in the foreword, I am FAR from perfect.

References

All articles are the personal creation of Barry M. Holcomb. Most of the works contained in this volume have been printed previously in newspapers. Some articles appeared on the internet as part of a weekly column at the website RuntimeDNA.com and are listed below. Some articles are appearing in print for the first time in this volume.

What's in Your Medicine Chest, *The Westmoreland News*, Montross, VA.

Of Gardens and Tillers, *The Beacon*, Selma, Al.

Touch of a Loving Hand, *Living with Preschoolers*, The Broadman Press, 1986.

It's a Girl, *The Clinton Chronicle*, Clinton, SC, 1983.

The Broken Camera, *The Beacon*, Selma, AL.

The Camel's Final Journey, *The Westmoreland News*, Montross, VA.

My Snowglobe on the Shelf, *The Westmoreland News*, Montross, VA.

Christmas Came a Little Early this Year, *The Westmoreland News*, Montross, VA.

Inspiration Point, *The Beacon*, Selma, AL.

The Search, *The Clinton Chronicle*, Clinton, SC.

When Will Christmas Come Again, *The Clinton Chronicle*, Clinton, SC.

The Old Man and the Lake, *The Westmoreland News*, Montross, VA.

Daddy Versus GE, *The Westmoreland News*, Montross, VA.

Make a Memory (Retitled Moveable Feasts), *The Westmoreland News,* Montross, VA.

Not Your Usual Tourist, *The Westmoreland News*, Montross, VA. *The Beacon*, Selma, AL.

Not Just a Dog, *The Westmoreland News*, Montross, VA.

What Good is an Old Grouch? *The Westmoreland News*, Montross, VA.

Thank You, Miss Frances. The Westmoreland News, Montross, VA.

Photographs are taken from the personal collection of Barry M. Holcomb. Some photos were taken by Michael G. Brooks and are used with permission.

The Epilogue bears the 3D image *Enter Into* by Michael Brooks. The Publicity Department of Tweetsie Railroad provided the photo of the engine crossing the trestle.

The following articles appeared on the website RuntimeDNA.com

Of Gardens and Tillers

The Camel's Final Journey

My Snowglobe on the Shelf

The Birdnest Symposium

The Hero in the Common Man

Inspiration Point

My Own Private Gallery

The Right Tool for the Job

The Song Indescribable

Spring Fever

The Light in Willie's Eyes

Treading on Holy Ground

Food of the Gods

Magical Train Ride

The Old Man and the Lake

Daddy Vs GE

Make a Memory

The Honey-Do List

I Thought of you Today, Mama

A Lifetime of Chocolate Bunnies

Not Just a Dog

A Gift from Heaven

Strangle that Bird!

Thank you, Miss Frances

Did you Hear That?

God DOES Have a Sense of Humor

Where DO Grits Come From?

About the Author

Barry Holcomb grew up in the small town of Clinton, South Carolina. "We had more than 3 stoplights in town, but just a few more." Growing nostalgic about the past he describes Clinton as the kind of town "where little old ladies pull into the middle of an intersection and stop. Then they look both ways before continuing through."

Even as a youngster, Barry worked at his father's business, seeing on a daily basis the differences and the sameness of people, and learning the humor of life.

After completing studies at Presbyterian College, he worked for 9 years in the Special Education field. Moving to Charlotte with his family, he went into the fast-food industry where he worked for 25 years.

Barry is now retired and enjoys spending time with his two children and one grandson who all live nearby.

Made in the USA
Charleston, SC
18 February 2015